UNCOMMON VALOR

Insignia of the NYPD Emergency Service Unit

ANDREW G. NELSON

Copyright © 2015 by Andrew G. Nelson

All rights reserved. This book, or parts thereof, may not be reproduced, distributed, or transmitted in any form, or by any means, or stored in a database or retrieval system, without prior written permission.

Cover Design Copyright © 2015 by Huntzman Enterprises

Published by Huntzman Enterprises

Huntzman Enterprises
Edinburg, IL. 62531

First Printing: July 2015

ISBN-10: 0996133437
ISBN-13: 978-0-9961334-3-2

Printed in the United States of America
1 3 5 7 9 10 8 6 4 2

Other Titles by

Andrew G. Nelson

<u>James Maguire Series</u>

Perfect Pawn

Queen's Gambit

Bishop's Gate

<u>Alex Taylor Series</u>

Small Town Secrets

DEDICATION

To my wife Nancy, without your love, support and constant encouragement this book would not have been possible. Thank you for always believing in me.

To Chuck, whose guidance and friendship fueled my appreciation for the history of the job. You are missed every day. Fidelis Ad Mortem, my friend.

To the men and women of the NYPD ESU: The epitome of NY's Finest.

And to God, through whom all things are possible.

Romans 8:28

ACKNOWLEDGEMENTS

The book you hold in your hand is the culmination of a research project that began in early 2011. What started out as a simple idea, turned into a process that was both exhilarating and frustrating, often at the same time.

It is not enough to just present a collection of items for the reader to ogle over. It is the people and the stories behind the insignia that are the crucial component; those who have designed and worn their emblems with honor.

In researching the material for this book I discovered a number of amazing stories, which would only have been possible through the assistance of a great many people, including numerous members of ESU, both active and retired. They provided me with not only a treasure trove of information, but something equally as precious: their time.

I would like to take this moment to extend my sincere thanks to the following:

Names Appear in Alphabetical Order

Patrick Barry, Chris Begg, Andy Bershad, Mike Bosak, Dave Brink, Carol D'Allara, Mike Fanning, Frank Ferrara, Frank Gallagher, Robert Gardella, Al Gut, Brian Hearn, Rob Isernia, Glenn Klein, Chuck Kobel, Todd Lamison, Tony Lisi, Tom Longa, Vinny Manco, Tony Mangiaracina, Rick Martinez, Scott Mateyaschuk, Kristie Maryou, James McCafferty, Stuart McConnell, Lenny Mendel, Al Mendez, Sean Mulcahy, Tom Murphy, Tom O'Connor, Vinny Papasodero, George Pillion, Pat Pogan, Roger Savage, Evan Schwerner, Al Sheppard, Joe Sede, Bob Sivori, David Smith, David Smith (*Phoenix Sign*), Dave Smutek, Ed Vanderberg, Kathy Vigiano, Brian Wall, Brandon Watson, & Pete Whalen

IN MEMORIUM

The first recorded ESU officer who died in the line of duty was Patrolman William Kertin, ESU Squad 1. He was killed on July 28th, 1929 from injuries he sustained in an auto accident. The ESU truck that he was riding in had been responding to an alarm, when it struck a bus. Kertin was killed and four other ESU officers were injured.

At the time of this 1st printing there have been a total of thirty-five (35) ESU officers who have died as a result of injuries sustained in the line of duty. This number includes the fourteen (14) who were killed in the terrorist attack at the World Trade Center on September 11th, 2001.

It should be noted that the last five officers listed below died as a result of illnesses directly attributed to the September 11th attack. Sadly, it is a cruel reality that the lingering health issues from that event will continue to claim victims, well into the future.

In researching the material for this book I was struck by the number of officers who had been involved in the design of their respective unit's insignia and had died in the line of duty.

I think it is fitting that this book honors not only them, but every ESU officer who has paid the ultimate price. Their sacrifice is the embodiment of the NYPD Motto: *Fidelis Ad Mortem* (Latin for: Faithful Unto Death).

- Ptl. William A. Kertin – July 28th, 1929
- Sgt. George Nadler – February 1st, 1935
- Ptl. Joseph J. McBreen – August 11th, 1937
- Ptl. Alexander C. Stutt – June 9th, 1939
- Ptl. Francis M. O'Hara – November 25th, 1946
- Ptl. Peter J. Knudsen – November 25th, 1946
- Lt. Charles R. Michie – November 25th, 1946

- Ptl. Charles A. Brereton – September 30th, 1947
- Ptl. Kenneth L. Cozier – April 19th, 1963
- Ptl. John Banks – April 15th, 1968
- Ptl. Salvatore Spinola – October 2nd, 1969
- Ptl. Patrick O'Connor – November 24th, 1971
- P.O. Stephen Gilroy – January 19th, 1973
- P.O. Joseph McCormack – September 29th, 1983
- P.O. Francis LaSala – January 10th, 1987
- Sgt. John Coughlin – September 11th, 2001
- Sgt. Rodney Gillis – September 11th, 2001
- Sgt. Michael Curtin – September 11th, 2001
- P.O. Jerome Dominguez – September 11th, 2001
- P.O. Walter Weaver – September 11th, 2001
- P.O. Ronald Kloepfer – September 11th, 2001
- P.O. Thomas Langone – September 11th, 2001
- P.O. Vincent Danz – September 11th, 2001
- P.O. Joseph Vigiano – September 11th, 2001
- P.O. Stephen Driscoll – September 11th, 2001
- P.O. Santos Valentin – September 11th, 2001
- P.O. Paul Talty – September 11th, 2001
- P.O. John D'Allara – September 11th, 2001
- P.O. Brian McDonnell – September 11th, 2001
- Sgt. Keith Ferguson – January 31st, 2004
- Capt. Barry Galfano – June 26th, 2011 *
- Lt. Christopher Pupo – June 23rd, 2012 *
- Capt. Dennis Morales – July 27th, 2012 *
- P.O. Anthony Mangiaracina – September 10th, 2012 *
- Sgt. Patrick P. Murphy – August 20th, 2014 *

* Was a Member of ESU at the time of the 9/11 attack and developed illness as a result of that assignment.

TABLE OF CONTENTS

1. FOREWORD
2. INTRODUCTION
3. REGULATION PATCHES
4. VEST PATCHES
5. BDU PATCHES
6. TOMCAT – THE BIRTH OF A MASCOT
7. TRUCK PATCHES

    - TRUCK ONE (MANHATTAN)
    - TRUCK TWO (MANHATTAN)
    - TRUCK THREE (BRONX)
    - TRUCK FOUR (BRONX)
    - TRUCK FIVE (STATEN ISLAND)
    - TRUCK SIX (BROOKLYN)
    - TRUCK SEVEN (BROOKLYN)
    - TRUCK EIGHT (BROOKLYN)
    - TRUCK NINE (QUEENS)
    - TRUCK TEN (QUEENS)

8. OTHER UNITS
    - A-TEAM / CAT
    - SNIPER
    - WMD / HAMMER
    - EMERGENCY MEDICAL SQUAD / TAC MEDIC
    - K9
    - FEMA NYTF-1

9. EVENTS & MISCELLANEOUS
10. NYC HOUSING – EMERGENCY RESCUE UNIT
11. NYC TRANSIT – EMERGENCY MEDICAL RESCUE UNIT

FOREWORD

"*When the public needs help they call the police, when the police need help they call ESU.*"

I first started collecting police insignia, as a rookie NYPD officer, back in 1986. But the first police insignia I ever received predated that by another dozen and a half years at least. My law enforcement career, my collecting *bug*, and my name for that matter can all be traced back to my maternal grandfather, James A. Maguire, or Andy, as he was known to family and friends alike.

He was a truck driver and foreman for a company in the Jamaica area of Queens which is in the confines of the 103rd Precinct. Back in the 70's, when the city was facing ever worsening fiscal woes, they began laying off police officers. My grandfather tried to take care of the local guys, *hooking them up* as the saying goes, with side jobs to help them out. He had always wanted to be a cop and, while he had the *Irish* part going for him, it didn't make up for the height requirement which he was lacking in. However, that didn't stop him from making friends with a lot of police officers.

This was back in the 60's and 70's and the world, in so far as policing went, was a much different place. I remember many occasions when the doorbell would ring in the 3rd floor apartment where my grandparents lived. As the door opened there would be cops clad in leather jackets standing there. They would walk into the apartment and, after exchanging pleasantries with my grandmother, they would retire with my grandfather to the living room to *visit*.

During those years I recall getting little trinkets from most of those officers. One time it would be a tie clip, another time a pair of collar brass. Once I even got a mini police officer's shield.

Somewhere along the line I got an ESU patch. Over time, and several moves, most of the metal stuff got lost, but the ESU patch I still have.

The men and women of ESU are some of the bravest and most professional cops you will ever encounter. It is also not unusual that they are among the most decorated officers in the NYPD. The accolades and awards only serve to reflect the extremely dangerous job that they perform on the mean streets of New York City, each and every day. They truly do possess: *Uncommon Valor.*

As a kid, my heroes were always cops. As a cop, my heroes were *E-Men*!

No other unit of the New York City Police Department has a history as long and storied as the Emergency Service Unit.

From that first ESU patch came the foundations of a hobby that would last well into my retirement. I am equally proud of both my career and my collection. In 1986 I had the good fortune to be introduced to another police officer, Charles 'Chuck' Kobel.

Chuck was a cop's cop. A member of the Mounted Unit and who had been awarded the department's Medal for Valor. We became fast friends and he took on the role as my mentor, schooling me on the history of NYPD insignia. He was a historian, someone who looked beyond the actual patch, at the history of each individual piece.

It was from that foundation that I came to realize that we are nothing more than *caretakers* of an item; handing it off, when the time comes, to the next generation of collectors. I have also learned that it is not enough to pass along the item, but we must preserve the history as well. Otherwise, it is nothing more than an ornate piece of cloth.

In 2002, my hobby merged with the production side. My wife started her own business doing insignia design work and, over the years, we have produced dozens of patches and coins for the Emergency Service Unit. While I knew the history of the insignia we have made, I had a number of questions about the older ones.

That was my purpose for writing this book. To ensure that future generations of collectors would have access to this information. It has been a painstaking journey as I tried to weed out the facts from the fiction.

I am proud to present to you this undertaking: Uncommon Valor - Insignia of the NYPD Emergency Service Unit.

Sgt. Andrew G. Nelson, NYPD (Ret.)
Edinburg, Illinois – June 2015

INTRODUCTION

In 1964, the Philadelphia Police Department established what became known as the *first* official Special Weapons and Tactics (SWAT) team in the United States. Three years later, the Los Angeles Police Department launched their SWAT team. These were the first units dedicated to specifically addressing escalating violence in urban areas. Without taking anything away from these two premier agencies, in my opinion they were about four decades late to the party.

In April 1930, the New York City Police Department's, Emergency Service Division (ESD), was *officially* created. I say that because, while the Division was started on that date, the foundation of the Police Emergency Service can actually be traced back several years earlier to 1925.

In fact, if one were to look at the history in totality, one can follow a lineage that goes back to the days of the old Police Reserve Squads, which were formed after the American Civil War to deal with riots. These reserves consisted of officers who were assigned *extra duty* to supplement the regular patrol force, in the event of a public disturbance.

After WWI, a growing climate of social unrest led to rioting in more than three dozen U.S. cities in the summer of 1919. It revealed the need for a specialized, highly trained, unit to respond to these events. This led to the creation of the NYPD's Riot Battalion. The personnel of the Riot Battalion, also sometimes referred to as the *Riot Regiment*, was composed of members of the Police Department who had actual military experience, and who were thoroughly versed in the handling and use of firearms, as well as various other implements of warfare.

As originally conceived, the Riot Battalion consisted of four companies: 'A', 'B', 'C', and 'D'. Each company was headed by a

Captain, 3 Lieutenants, 7 Sergeants and 104 Patrolmen. During the era of Prohibition, a 'Machine Gun' Company was added, and was staffed with a Captain, 4 Sergeants and 72 Patrolmen. Its primary role was addressing the rise in organized crime activity, including illegal breweries.

As time progressed, the need for a unit focused primarily on riots and crowd control began to diminish. A steadily growing population, coupled with increases in urban construction and a diversifying system of transportation, began to present new issues that the regular patrol officers simply could not begin to handle effectively. It soon became obvious that there was a need to have a specialized unit, which would be available to respond to the new type of emergency situations that New York City was beginning to face.

Police officers were now being forced to contend with a myriad of issues, such as gas leaks, pedestrians being run over by vehicles or falling from elevated train lines, and horses that would fall into open construction sites. As a result, protocols were developed that directed the reserve officers of the Riot Battalions to respond to these types of emergency calls, when they were not assigned to riot or crowd control duties.

This program proved to be so effective, that on July 7th, 1925, New York City Police Commissioner Richard E. Enright issued a formal order establishing two dedicated 'Emergency Automobile Squads'. Enright authorized the purchase of two, custom built, 1925 White Motor Company trucks.

These vehicles were equipped with all the necessary equipment to handle any emergency which might occur. The original trucks were enamel blue in color and had the lettering 'EMERGENCY SERVICE' written in gold lettering on the side.

White Motor Co. Truck circa late 1920's.

The Emergency Automobile Squad combined the duties of a rescue unit, *Pulmotor* (Oxygen) truck, riot platoon, first-aid, and motorized patrol. Each squad was designated to respond to all fires of two alarms or more, riots, train wrecks, serious automobile collisions, and any other emergencies where there were serious injuries or people were likely to die.

Initially, the coverage of the city was divided up amongst the two squads, which were comprised of six sergeants and forty-four officers.

While the original recommendation was for a lieutenant to be in charge of each squad, there are no personnel records of any lieutenants actually being transferred into Emergency Service until the division was formed in 1930.

- Emergency Automobile Squad #1 was quartered at 138 West 30th Street in Manhattan and was assigned to respond to emergencies in the boroughs of Manhattan and the Bronx. The officers reported to, and were under the supervision of, the Commanding Officer of the 7th Precinct.

- Emergency Automobile Squad #2 was quartered in Brooklyn at 298 Classon Avenue and was assigned to respond to emergencies in the boroughs of Brooklyn and Queens. The officers reported to, and were under the supervision of, the Commanding Officer of the 46th Precinct.

The following list contains the names of the original fifty members of the Emergency Automobile Squad, as established by NYPD Special Order #171 dated 07/06/1925:

Emergency Automobile #1

Sergeant:

Sgt. James M. Gordon Jr.
Sgt. Joseph A. Stanton
Sgt. John F. Ward

Patrolmen:

William J. Bak
Otto W. Behrens
John J. Boyle
Frank A. Dineen
Daniel J. Flynn
Henry Fleuchaus
John J. Hartnett
James A. Irving Jr.
Frederick Kahrig
William Kaval
Daniel F. Kerrigan
Francis M. Kelly
Albert E. Latchford
George C. Moench
John D. Paar
Frederick L. Pfeiffer
Edward F. Powers
Frederick H. Sorger
Laurence H. Spitzen
Joseph Theuer
John Tormey

Emergency Automobile #2

Sergeant:

Sgt. Ulysses E. Beotig
Sgt. David Geraghty
Sgt. Joseph Green

Patrolmen:

Ernest M. Emann
Charles Frailer
John J. Hartnett
James F. O'Brien
Francis J. Donnelly
Charles Dosch
Joseph V. DeSoucey
William Ferri
Michael P. Higgins
Edward O. Junginger
Charles P. Klein
Charles E. Kraemer
Walter G. Lagarenne
Edward B. Lahey
Edwin L. Lundin
Joseph F. Motjenbacker
Ernest Peters
Edward F. Powers
Thomas C. Regan
John M. Simerlein
Arthur F. Walz
Albert L. Williamson
Edward Unger

On September 16th, 1926, based upon the success of the inaugural two Emergency Automobile Squads, Police Commissioner George McLaughlin ordered that a third squad, comprised of three sergeants and nineteen officers, be organized and put into service. The name of the unit was also officially changed from the Emergency Automobile Squad to the Emergency Service Squad.

- Emergency Service Squad #3 was quartered in the Bronx at 820 Washington Avenue and was assigned to respond to emergencies in the Bronx. The officers reported to the Commanding Officer of the 19th Pct.

On November 3rd, 1926, the officers of Emergency Service engaged in their first major gun battle when NYC mobster, Herman 'Hyman' Amberg, who was in jail for the murder of a local jeweler, attempted to escape from the old 'Tombs' jail on Centre Street, along with two other prisoners. Pistols had been previously smuggled into the jail for the three men. They faked illnesses so that they would be brought to the jail doctor. Once inside the doctor's office, they pulled their guns and attempted to escape. Newly assigned Warden, Peter Mallon, heard the commotion and came running to stop the escape. He was shot and killed as he entered the office.

The three inmates then fled into the prison courtyard, near the Lafayette Street gate, where they exchanged shots with Keeper (the former title for Corrections Officer) Jeremiah Murphy and his partner, Daniel O'Connor. Keeper Murphy was killed and his partner was wounded.

Emergency Service responded and engaged the inmates from nearby buildings, raking the jail from all sides with heavy machine gun fire and gas bombs.

The gun battle at the Tombs went on for thirty minutes, with hundreds of rounds being fired. Amberg and the other two inmates hunkered down behind a pile of coal in the yard, before making their way to the safety of a guardhouse. They occasionally returned fire, wounding a police officer and a businessman in the Conklin Building across the street. At some point, two of the inmates were shot and wounded. With no escape possible, all three committed suicide.

On May 4th, 1928, Police Commissioner Joseph A. Warren, issued General Order #11 which doubled the number of squads in service, creating new Squads 4, 5 & 6. Each squad was manned by three sergeants and twenty-one officers.

This expansion resulted in a redistricting of the service areas for these units, as well as a relocation of quarters for Squad #2. These squads, and their vehicles, were assigned to the following precincts:

- Emergency Squad #1 was quartered in the 7th Precinct at 138 West 30th Street in Manhattan. It was assigned to respond to emergencies in Manhattan, south of 86th Street, including all of Central Park and the Borough of Richmond.

- Emergency Squad #2 was relocated to the 15th Precinct, at 1854 Amsterdam Avenue in Manhattan. It was assigned to respond to emergencies in Manhattan, north of 86th Street, excluding of Central Park.

- Emergency Squad #3 was quartered in the 19th Precinct at 3rd Avenue and 160th Street in the Bronx. It was assigned to respond to all emergencies in the Bronx.

- Emergency Squad #4 (Formerly Squad 2) was quartered in the 42-A Precinct, located at 653 Grand Avenue in Brooklyn. It was assigned to respond to all emergencies in Brooklyn, except within the boundaries of the 44th, 48-A, 49th, 49-A, 50th, 51st, and 51-A Precincts.

- Emergency Squad #5 was quartered in the 59th Precinct Station House, located at 85 Fourth Street, Long Island City, Queens. It was assigned to respond to all emergencies in the 59th and 64th Precincts in Queens as well as the 48-A, 49th, 49-A, 50th, 51st, and 51-A Precincts in Brooklyn.

- Emergency Squad #6 was quartered in the 56th Precinct at 275 Church Street in Richmond Hill, Queens. It was assigned to respond to all emergencies in Queens, except the 59th and 64th Precincts, as well as the 44th Precinct in Brooklyn.

POLICE DEPARTMENT
CITY OF NEW YORK
OFFICE OF THE POLICE COMMISSIONER

New York, May 4, 1928.

GENERAL ORDERS NO. 11.

POLICE EMERGENCY SERVICE

General Orders No. 26, 1926, is hereby amended to read:

1. Police Emergency Service is hereby established, and shall consist of automobiles with emergency equipment and trained crews. This service is established for the purpose of getting members of the Force of this Department to the scene of an emergency in the shortest time possible to establish police lines and perform such other duty as may be required at large fires, riots, strikes or catastrophies. The Police Emergency Service Squads, when on duty, must at all times be prepared to respond instantly.

2. Upon arriving at the scene of an emergency the commanding officer of the Police Emergency Service Squad will immediately establish police lines, take charge of and be responsible for the distribution of all members of the Force who respond to the emergency until the arrival of an officer of higher rank. He will immediately inform the commanding officer of the Telegraph Bureau of the nature of the occurrence and the number of additional reserves required, if any.

3. The commanding officer at the scene of an emergency will release the Police Emergency Squad as soon as their services can be dispensed with, promptly notifying the Telegraph Bureau of such action. The commanding officer of the Police Emergency Squad will immediately notify the Telegraph Bureau of their return to quarters.

4. The Police Emergency Service will be installed in the following precincts and will be an integral part of such commands, and will cover the territory specified:

Police Emergency Service No. 1.
7th Precinct, 138 West 30th Street, Manhattan

All that territory within the Borough of Manhattan, south of 86th Street, including Central Park, and the Borough of Richmond.

Police Emergency Service No. 2
15th Precinct, 1854 Amsterdam Avenue, Manhattan

All that territory within the Borough of Manhattan, north of 86th Street, except Central Park.

Police Emergency Service No. 3
19th Precinct, 3d Avenue and 160th Street, The Bronx

All that territory within the Borough of The Bronx.

Police Emergency Service No. 4

42-A Precinct, 653 Grand Avenue, Borough of Brooklyn

All that territory within the Borough of Brooklyn, except within the boundaries of the 44th, 48-A, 49th, 49-A, 50th, 51st and 51-A Precincts.

Police Emergency Service No. 5

59th Precinct, 85 Fourth Street, Long Island City, Queens

All that territory within the 59th and 64th Precincts, Borough of Queens, and that within the boundaries of the 48-A, 49th, 49-A, 50th, 51st and 51-A Precincts, Borough of Brooklyn.

Police Emergency Service No. 6

56th Precinct, 275 Church Street, Richmond Hill, Queens

All that territory within the 44th Precinct, Borough of Brooklyn, and all of the Borough of Queens, except that within the boundaries of the 59th and 64th Precincts.

5. A sergeant designated by the Police Commissioner shall be in command of each Police Emergency Service Squad.

6. The force assigned to each such Police Emergency Service will be known as the Police Emergency Service Squad and will work according to the regular Patrolmen's Duty Chart. Sergeants in command of Police Emergency Service No. 1 and No. 4 will be assigned to the 1st, 4th and 7th Squads, and Sergeants in command of Police Emergency Service No. 2 and No. 5 will be assigned to the 2d, 5th and 8th Squads, and Sergeants in command of Police Emergency Service No. 3 and No. 6 will be assigned to the 3d, 6th and 9th squads. At least two patrolmen of the Police Emergency Service Squad will be assigned to each squad of the Patrolmen's Duty Chart. Vacancies will be filled as provided by the Rules and Regulations. Assignments to the Police Emergency Service will not be changed for any reason, except with the approval of the Police Commissioner.

7. Commanding Officers of precincts to which this emergency service is assigned will provide necessary accomodations for the automobile and squads.

8. A blotter will be kept in which will be entered all calls and all active police duty performed by the Police Emergency Service Squads. This does not include roll calls, etc., which will be kept in the Precinct Blotter.

9. These Police Emergency Service Automobiles with crews will proceed to the scene of any Police Emergency as directed by the Chief Inspector, or Deputy Chief Inspector at Police Headquarters. They will also proceed to the scene of fires on second alarms received from fire signal stations. They will answer first alarms only when so directed.

10. The Fire Department call for Police Emergency Service will be a preliminary ten strokes, followed by ten strokes, followed by the fire station number where desired, followed by the number of the Police Emergency Service wanted.

Effective 8 A. M., May 5, 1928.

JOSEPH A. WARREN,
Police Commissioner.

On April 10th, 1930, Police Commissioner Grover A. Whalen issued General Order #20, which created the Emergency Service Division. The individual units were removed from the control of the precinct commanders and transferred under the command of Inspector Daniel A. Kerr, the first commanding officer of the division.

Inspector Kerr, also known as 'Iron Dan', held the distinction of being the strongest man in the NYPD. Kerr won the title after emerging victorious from a wrestling match against fellow officer, and former professional weightlifter, Selig "Ajax" Whitman.

At the time, Kerr wanted to get away from what he perceived to be the more *violent* chapters of the unit's history in dealing with riots. He envisioned a more service oriented unit and created the axiom '*At Your Service*'. Over the years, this saying faded away, replaced with the more appropriate: '*Anytime, Anywhere, Any Place*'.

By this time the number of Emergency Service Squads had been increased from six to twenty. In June of 1930, ESD commenced its own emergency service school at the police academy. This two week intense course was designed to prepare incoming members for the rigors of Emergency Service work.

By the mid 1930's, the division had also absorbed the Aviation Bureau and Harbor Unit, giving it a unique *land*, *sea* and *air* capability. By the early 1950's the division would reduce the number of squads by half, resulting in the current 10 Squad structure that remains in place today.

Over time, the nomenclature would change from Emergency Service Division (ESD) to Emergency Service Section (ESS) and finally to Emergency Service Unit (ESU).

In June 1973, both the Aviation and Harbor units became autonomous entities. That same year saw the first female officer, Ann Morrissey, a nursing specialist, assigned to ESU.

The next major change in ESU occurred in 1995, when the NYC Housing and Transit Police Departments were merged into the NYPD. With this merger, the personnel of the HAPD and TAPD Emergency Rescue Units were absorbed into ESU.

One of the aspects which set ESU apart from other tactical units around the country is the fact that the officers of ESU are tasked with responding to every conceivable emergency situation. They are called upon to handle everything from plane crashes and building collapses, to persons threatening to jump from bridges. There simply are no *typical* days for ESU officers. They have literally seen and done everything.

When an officer on patrol encounters something he can't handle, the call goes out to send ESU. On any given day ESU officers can go from a *pin job*, a motor vehicle accident with a person trapped inside, to an armed barricaded emotionally disturbed person. The vehicles they travel in contain equipment that make them look like a mobile version of *Home Depot* and *Guns-R-Us*.

The training program for ESU officers includes the following:

- Bridge & Building Rescues
- Vehicle & Train Accident Extrication
- Building Collapse Extrication
- Rigging & Line Techniques
- Welding / Torch Techniques
- First Aid / Emergency Medical Technician
- Non-Lethal Weapons
- Power Tool Operation
- Elevator / Escalator Rescue
- Animal Control
- Water Rescue
- Helicopter Rescue / Rappel / Medevac
- Bomb / IED Recognition

- HAZMAT / Chemical Agents
- Dignitary Protection Operations
- Specialized Vehicle Operations
- Hostage Rescue
- Emotionally Disturbed Persons
- SCUBA
- Electrical / Gas Emergencies
- Aircraft Emergency / Rescue
- Forcible / Barricaded Entry Techniques
- High Rise Structure Rescues
- Department of Correction Emergencies
- Self-Contained Breathing Apparatus
- Auxiliary Generators / Lighting
- Specialized Weapons Training

All of this, while still maintaining a routine patrol function.

Today, the Emergency Service Unit is divided into ten *trucks*, the name colloquially used to describe the ten individual commands which are tasked with providing coverage throughout the five boroughs of New York City.

- Truck 1 (Manhattan)
- Truck 2 (Manhattan)
- Truck 3 (Bronx)
- Truck 4 (Bronx)
- Truck 5 (Staten Island)
- Truck 6 (Brooklyn)
- Truck 7 (Brooklyn)
- Truck 8 (Brooklyn)
- Truck 9 (Queens)
- Truck 10 (Queens)

Each of these commands use two distinct types of vehicles. The large 'Truck', which usually remains at the quarters unless summoned for a big job, and three smaller Radio Emergency

Patrol vehicles, or *REP*'s. These smaller trucks are used for routine patrol and initial emergency response. Their radio call signs are 'Adam', 'Boy', and 'Charlie'.

Photo courtesy of Tom O'Connor

REGULATION ESU PATCH

The regulation patch of the Emergency Service Unit has remained relatively unchanged throughout the unit's long history. However, I would be remiss if I didn't tell you that trying to pin a particular design down to an actual date, when it was either first worn or discontinued, can sometimes be an effort in futility. When it comes to the regulation insignia it is best to break it down to a general time period (i.e. mid 1970's).

The reason for this vagueness is that just because a particular style was discontinued didn't mean that it was no longer used. In some cases it is not uncommon to find round patches being worn long after the changeover period. The simple explanation for this is that cops tend to use something till it is no longer serviceable. If a shirt is still good, they will still wear it, regardless of what patch is worn. In addition, some patches are seen as a *badge of honor* denoting older veterans from the *new guys*.

While I was researching this book, I would encounter two mysteries that reaffirmed for me the importance of why I was pursuing this endeavor.

The first mystery occurred while I was researching the history of the NYPD's Aviation Unit's insignia. I was provided an article titled '*The Reminiscences of Arthur W. Wallender*'. The article, which dealt with the formation of the Aviation Bureau, featured a photo, dated October 24th, 1929, that showed the original nine applicants for the unit.

As I examined the photo I observed that one of the members was wearing what appeared to be a round ESU patch. Under a magnifying glass I could clearly see what appeared to me to be the hood cowling of the blue truck. At the time, the only unit that had anything remotely resembling this style was the Harbor patch, but that featured a fouled anchor, set at an angle, and none of these elements could be seen in the patch worn by the officer. In addition, the Harbor patch did not have a light colored border, which is clearly visible in the patch in the photo.

Original applicants for NYPD Aviation Bureau: October 24th, 1929.

In the NYPD collecting field, it was generally acknowledged that the round ESU patch came into existence sometime after April 1930 when the Division was officially created. Either the date of the photo was mislabeled, or the unit clearly had a patch much earlier than anyone had imagined.

In 1929, Arthur Wallender was a Captain and headed the Aviation Bureau. He would also serve as the C.O. of the Emergency Service Division from 1936-1938 and then as Police Commissioner from 1945-1949. It was highly unlikely that his recollection or the information on the photo was incorrect. Intrigued, I began looking deeper into this.

Further research determined that the date on the photo was correctly labeled. The first insignia used by Emergency Service actually dated back to over a year before the 'official' creation of the unit in April 1930. It also would answer one of the nagging questions I had always had about the ESU patch, which was: *why is the truck blue?*

Many historians point to the original ESU truck as being a 1930 Mack truck. As noted earlier, I had discovered that the original two 1925 White Motor Company trucks, purchased by the department, were in fact blue in color. So in 1929, this would have been the color scheme in use, as the green Mack trucks did not come about until 1930.

In February 14th, 1929, the approved Emergency Service patch, was designed by Peter Hewitson of Glendale, Queens, and was selected from a total of three designs.

Hewitson, who was also known as *'Grover Whalen, Jr.'*, was the Department's *mascot* in the mid 20's. Sadly, the other two designs which were submitted for consideration remain lost to time.

Hewitson's design consisted of a small, roughly 2.75" round, dark blue wool patch which was worn on the dress jacket.

In the center was the original blue White Motor Co. truck with yellow rails and white tires. On the top was the word 'Emergency' and on bottom 'Squad' in red. The border of the patch was done in the same blue color as the truck.

According to the news reports, Hewitson remarked that he had used that particular lettering so that "no one would mistake the squad for being furniture bill collectors."

These patches were worn on the left uniform sleeve just above the elbow. Because the design remained the same for decades, it is not uncommon to find minor manufacturers variations in detailing, color and material.

Older style patch being worn in late 1940's

Later, issues of the jacket patch appeared with a dark blue *felt* material backing.

In addition to the jacket patches, there were two other versions produced for wear on other garments.

One patch, a light blue denim style, was said to have been worn on coveralls in the late 40's. The other version, done in a twill material, was worn on uniform shirts into the 70's.

As with the jacket patch, because of the number of different manufacturers, it is not uncommon to run into numerous variations of the shirt patch.

MASCOT'S ART WINS ON POLICE INSIGNIA

Pete Hewitson, or "Grover Whalen Jr.," Takes Prize for Emergency Squad Tinsel

DIDN'T USE "DRAG," EITHER

In one of the most hotly contested art competitions in the Centre and Broome Streets art colony, Pete Hewitson—"Grover Whalen Jr." they call him around Police Headquarters—learned today his design for the sleeve insignia of the Police Emergency Squad has been officially approved.

There were three designs submitted, but Pete's won. There were whispers that Pete, who is nineteen, a former mascot of the department, used undue influence to get his design over.

"That's a lot of asparagus," Pete said today. "If I had wanted to use pull I'd have got Al Smith to say a word for me. I used to be Al's bodyguard."

Pete produced an autograph book showing this notation: "To my bodyguard, Pete. Alfred E. Smith."

Sure, He Saved Smith

The former Governor wrote that back in 1924, at the Democratic convention in Madison Square Garden. Pete really was the Governor's messenger boy. But, if you listen to him, he saved Mr. Smith from bodily injury at the hands of Southern Democrats.

Pete's arm insignia for the six emergency squads of twenty-four men each consists of a silk-embroidered police truck in blue with hand rail in gold and the letters in red: "Emergency Squad," so nobody will suspect the squad of being furniture bill collectors.

Pete was the department's mascot from 1924 until 1926. He wore a captain's uniform and often traveled on beat with his police friends. To Pete a policeman is a god in No. 11's. And New York policemen are the salt of the earth.

"I'm anxious to get on the force myself," he admitted. "Only trouble is I'm 5 feet 8½ inches—I'm just an inch short of the regulations. Do you think I'll grow any more?"

Finds Police "Dolling Up"

"Grover Whalen Jr." was asked about his namesake.

"Who, the Commissioner? Oh, he's making out all right up there at headquarters. I hang around with the boys quite a bit, you know. They say Mr. Whalen is O. K. with them. One thing I've noticed—they're dressing up lots more since he came to headquarters. They're dolling up all the time now. A New York cop when he's dressed up is the swellest bird in town."

Pete lives at 135 Freemont Place, Glendale, Queens. His mother is always glad to see him drop in now and then. If she really wants him, she knows she can always telephone Police Headquarters.

She doesn't worry about her Pete. He's always in safe hands. He's always with his friends, the policemen.

New York Evening Post: February 14th, 1929

The second mystery I encountered occurred in the spring of 2012, when I was sent a photograph by a fellow collector asking me what patch I thought was being worn on the jacket sleeve at the scene of the Holland Tunnel explosion.

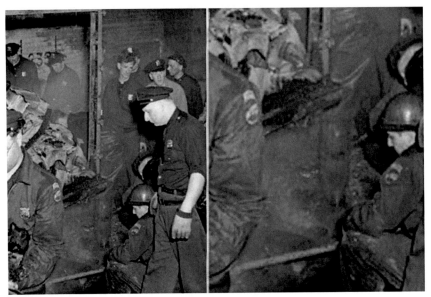

Holland Tunnel explosion: May 13th, 1949.

The image showed what appeared to be the ESU patch with the lettering "POLICE" on top. The only problem was, up until that time, it was believed by most collectors that the patch with the police tab didn't start being worn until the 70's.

This began a period of frantic research and emails to a number of retired E-Men. I'll never forget the shock when I got a reply back from Al Sheppard, a retired member of Truck 1 and author of the book: *E-Man, Life in the NYPD Emergency Service Unit*. Al informed me that, in addition to the round patch, there was also a separate patch which was produced exclusively for wear on the *Sweetore* work jackets.

This 3.25", partially embroidered patch, seen on the right, featured the traditional round design, but had a tab on the top that read 'Police' in white lettering. It was constructed of a heavy twill material and also had a knife-cut edge.

He said that in the 50's his uncle was a Sgt. in the ESD, assigned to mid-town, and stationed behind the 18th Pct. on West 54 St. He distinctly recalled seeing these patches being on the jackets at that time.

Al also shared a bit of Hollywood nostalgia on the topic of the work jackets. He informed me that in the original *King Kong* (1933) movie, there is an ESU truck in it. According to Al, if you slow the movie down, you can see the patch being worn by the ESU Sgt.

In addition, in the movie, *Emergency Squad* (1940), starring Anthony Quinn, it shows an ESU officer wearing the round patch on his shirt, and in another scene the patch with the 'Police' tab on a work jacket.

I admit that I have not seen either movie, but Al is a font of amazing ESU information and I have no reason to doubt the veracity of his movie trivia knowledge.

In light of what he told me, I began delving into older photos and immediately began to *see* the previously elusive patch being worn.

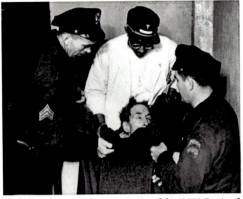

Over the course of my research I have found photographic evidence of this patch being worn back to the early 1940's.

Photo Courtesy of Kevin Reynolds, ESU Retired.

However, since the movie King Kong was done in 1933, I believe it is safe to say that this patch was being worn much earlier.

Photo Courtesy of Lenny Mendel, ESU Retired.

In the 1930's, and into the late 1940's, ESU Officers also wore a one-piece set of dark gray work coveralls. Affixed to the right breast and on either sleeve was a small, roughly 3.75" wide, dark grey, rectangular patch with the wording 'Police Emergency Squad' in red.

In the photo below, you can see the patches being worn on the left sleeve and right breast. Other photos from this time period show that the coverall patches were also worn on the right arm sleeve as well

Coverall patch being worn circa 1937.

This particular design seems to be the one most commonly encountered in period photographs. However, In addition to this style, there is another version that reads 'Police Emergency Squad 1'.

Unfortunately, because of the overall scarcity of these photos, none have surfaced so

far showing these numbered patches in use. It is believed that these would have mostly likely been worn in the early years of Emergency Service and it is conceivable that there could be upward of twenty different numbered variations.

In this photo, it does appear, based on the positioning of the letters, that there might have been a number under the word SQUAD at one time.

Perhaps the individual numbering was removed at a later date when the trucks were consolidated or maybe the officer was transferred to a new squad. Either way, by 1950, the use of the coveralls had been discontinued.

Another interesting bit of trivia was that during the 1939 / 40 World's Fair, held in Flushing Meadow Park in Queens, New York, members of the Emergency Service Division were assigned to the event. They wore the World's Fair patch as well as collar brass on their police uniform.

In 1971, the NYPD adopted its first regulation patch which was authorized for wear by all units on the right uniform sleeve, just below the shoulder.

The fully embroidered design incorporated the NYC city seal in the center, along with a white chevron containing five blue stars, one star for each of the city's five boroughs. Perched atop the chevron were the scales of justice. As with the other patches, it is not uncommon to encounter numerous variations of the current department patch.

The first version was approximately 4" in height and much narrower than the current 4.5" version that is used today. Both styles are depicted below.

In the early 1970's the use of the round ESU patch was dropped and the old work jacket style patch, with the "Police" tab, was adopted as the official ESU patch for wear on all uniforms.

The only modifications seemed to be the addition of a merrow style border. Unfortunately, the addition of this type of border made the round edges, of the bottom portion of the patch, appear straight.

Around 1976/77, ESU implemented the wearing of a baseball style cap instead of the traditional 8-point duty hat. At the time it was referred to as a *situational* hat, which was to take the place of the 8-point hat while on a job.

In the early 1980's, the patch underwent a minor alteration. While the overall design remained the same, the white lettering "NYPD" was added above the truck. This design remains in use today.

Throughout the years there have been a number of variations. Some have depicted the patch with a black background, while others appear to be missing some design elements, like the truck's windshield.

Most variations stem from the bidding process of low bid. This means that whichever company comes in the cheapest, gets the contract. This is done on all orders, so it is not uncommon to see a wide variety of insignia being used.

The two images below show a small sampling of the different manufacturer's variations of color and detail one might encounter.

In 2004, a set of subdued, fully embroidered, ESU and NYPD regulation patches were produced for a new, all-weather uniform trial. These patches were produced by *Huntzman Enterprises* and have the company's sticker on the reverse. They were to be sent to the uniform manufacturer so they could be applied before the uniforms were coated with *Scotch Guard* waterproofing.

You can see that a double border was added to the department patch, and the lower edges of the ESU patch were rounded a bit more, harkening back to the old style.

The concept behind the subdued patches was to separate ESU from the multitude of other departmental units who were now wearing the BDU styles uniforms.

While the subdued patches were ultimately rejected for the official uniform, they were later authorized for use by members of the Counter Sniper Team on the rain jackets.

They have also been used by members on their personal gear. The following are two examples of subdued patches attributed to the Counter Sniper Team.

Since the first set came out, in 2004, they have been reproduced by other vendors and it is not uncommon to find significant variations in the detailing.

In 2014, the department issued new tactical vests. These new vests now feature subdued insignia, including patches on both bicep protectors, which are affixed by Velcro.

The interesting thing is that both of these patches are only partially embroidered. The detailing is also a much lower quality than one would expect. I've included these vest patches here, as they are both regulation insignia, but I will cover the new breast and back patches worn on these new vests in a later chapter.

BDU PATCHES

In the beginning, ESU Officers traditionally wore the regulation uniform of the day. The only difference was the patch depicted on the arm. As the years progressed there were modifications to the uniform. Period photos show officers wearing the work jacket, along with what appears to be denim style pants. These changes were most likely brought about due to the detrimental effects of their daily work on the regulation uniforms.

In 1993, ESU switched from the traditional police uniform to a more practical military style BDU uniform which removed all of the metal insignia, including breast badges, medals, rank insignia and collar brass. This necessitated a new line of cloth insignia.

In addition to the color versions of the NYPD and ESU patches, the new uniforms featured patches on the back, breast and collar.

The partially embroidered back patches came in two versions. One that said NYPD in large letters and another that had the lettering POLICE in large letters.

Because these patches were private purchases, there were a number of variations based on vendors. While most of these measure in at roughly 9" wide, I have one version that is only 7.5" wide. Examples exist of both designs in either black or dark blue twill.

Along with the back patch was a partially embroidered breast patch, worn above the left pocket, which replaced the traditional metal shield. Again, because of different vendors, there are variations that can be found. While most are within the 4" wide range, I have seen others in the 5" wide range.

Above the right pocket was another patch. This partially embroidered patch, roughly 4" wide, featured the officer's name and shield number.

Additionally, the metal collar brass, which was used to denote assignment, was replaced as well with 1.5" wide, partially embroidered patch.

Originally, both collar patches had the lettering ESU on them. Later, it would be changed to denote the specific truck assignment. Each patch would have the letter "E" followed by the truck number that the officer was assigned to. Examples of these can be found as shown in the pictures below.

Again, it should be noted that it is not uncommon to find variations of the insignia above in both black and blue. You will also see that some of them also have a *dash* in between the letter and number. These patches have been around for over twenty years, as of this writing, and there are numerous vendors who have produced them.

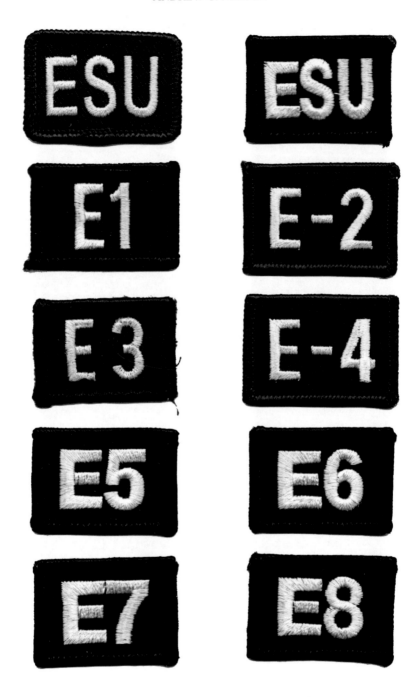

ESU members in the rank of Sergeant wear the traditional chevrons on both the right and left sleeves of their uniforms.

Members in the rank of Lieutenant and above also have corresponding cloth insignia that is worn on the collars. Two examples are shown below.

In addition to the above insignia, it is not all that uncommon to find other items, such as American flag patches and, in some instances, Blood Type patches being worn.

These appear to be a personal choice amongst the officers and are not considered official insignia. Flag patches are generally observed being worn on the upper left chest area of the tactical vest affixed by Velcro.

The two versions most often encountered are subdued patches, roughly 3.5" wide, with the lettering 'NYPD ESU' embroidered directly beneath it. Two examples are shown below.

VEST PATCHES

With the increased threat from larger caliber weapons, the members of ESU began wearing bullet resistent vests. This was before the advent of personal body armor.

These vests were worn over the standard uniform as seen in the photo to the right of two original members of the A-Team, Officer's Al Shepherd and Gary Gorman, who are also wearing the baseball caps.

Photo courtesy of Al Shepherd, ESU Retired

Later, patches were added to these vests to indicate that the wearer was the *police*. It seems a crazy thought, but somewhere, someone thought it appropriate. As if the mere site of uniformed men with guns drawn would cause some type of confusion.

The original 'heavy vests' were affixed with two separate 8.5" wide blue twill patches. 'POLICE' was worn on the front and 'Police Emergency NYPD' on the back.

In the early 1990's, there was a push to change the lettering from the traditional *NYPD* to *NYCPD*. As a result, changes began to pop up throughout the department. This even made an appearance on the vest patches. Like the BDU patches, all of these are partially embroidered.

Again, there were two different versions of the patch. The back patch was square in shape and roughly 8" wide. The breast patch, which also measured roughly 8", was more rectangular in size.

In the mid 1990's, this practice was reversed and the lettering again changed back to the traditional *NYPD*. As a result, the patches on the heavy vests were also changed.

Again, there were two different versions of these heavy vest patches. The back patch was square in shape and roughly 8" wide. The breast patch, which also measured roughly 8", was rectangular in shape.

Since there were multiple vendors used to produce these patches, it is not uncommon to find slight variations in sizes and colors.

It is hard to tell when one design was switched to another because they were worn as long as they were serviceable. Like the other patches, it is not uncommon to see period photos were both are being worn at the same time.

Another less often encountered vest patch is the one shown on the far right. This is referred to as the *Chinese vest* patch.

Here is the story as it was related to me by a retired ESU officer: *"We were fitted for this vest but the Chinese manufacturer cut them all for the same person. So we didn't have a lot of ballistic protection in the neckline to the middle of the chest and back. It was equivalent to wearing a ballistic wife-beater. The city being the city said 'too bad, wear the vest'. These were around for about 10 years until we got the new ones that they are wearing today. The patches were actually sewn directly into the vest pockets on the front and back so they couldn't be remove. In the end, most of these vests were either used up at the firearms range for testing or sent to Haiti."*

After the attacks of September 11th, the role of ESU took on another component, proactive counter terrorism. In response, members began utilizing military style *MOLLE* vests. On the front of the vest is a roughly 10" wide subdued patch that reads

POLICE in large letters. On the back is a similar size patch which reads NYPD-ESU. Unlike the previous style patches which were sewn on, these are attached via Velcro. However, it is not uncommon to find these switched from front to back as well.

In addition to the patches shown above, there are at least three others versions. One which reads CO ESU, another which reads XO ESU and a third which reads NYPD ESU K9.

In 2014, the department issued new heavy vests and plate carriers to ESU. In addition to the previously described subdued regulation and ESU patches being worn on the sleeves, the new vests also had new, subdued patches on the front and back, all affixed with Velcro.

On the front of the heavy vest is a 10.5" patch which reads: 'POLICE Emergency Service Unit'. On the back is a roughly 10.5" wide patch which reads: 'NYPD Emergency Service Unit'. This back patch is basically the same style back patch that is used on the BDU's, except the lettering is in a subdued grey color. Both patches also have Velcro backing.

The new plate carrier also features new patches. On the front of the carrier vest is a 4" wide patch which reads: 'NYPD Police Emergency Service Unit'. On the back is a roughly 9" wide patch which reads: 'NYPD Emergency Service Unit'. The edges of the back patch are cut at an angle to conform to the edges of the plate carrier.

The breast patch is basically the same style breast patch that is used on the BDU's, except the lettering is in a subdued grey color. Both patches also have Velcro backing.

As previously noted, the concept of ESU wearing subdued patches had always been balked at. However, in recent years it appears as if there has been a shift away from that viewpoint. It is therefore conceivable that, at some time in the near future, we may very well see ESU join the ranks of most other tactical units in wearing all subdued insignia on their uniforms.

TOMCAT – THE BIRTH OF A MASCOT

Nothing has come to symbolize ESU more than the Tomcat. With its cocky 'bring it on' grin and gun belt, you just knew it was ready for anything. Since the mid 80's, the Tomcat has appeared on more than twenty patches.

To fully appreciate the history of this iconic mascot, you have to look further back in time to the 1970's, when the Tomcat made its first appearance. The logo was actually co-opted from the Navy F-14 fighter jet program.

The birth of the Tomcat logo began when Dick Milligan, Director of Presentation Services, received a request from Norm Gandia, the Director of Grumman Business Development and a former No. 5 Blue Angel. Norm asked them to draw a lifelike Tomcat, wearing boxing gloves, trunks and sporting a six-shooter on his left side; where the guns are located on the F-14, along with two tails. The name 'Tom' was taken from then Chief of the Joint Chiefs of Staff, Thomas H. Moorer, and Chief of Naval Operations, Thomas F. Connolly.

One of the artists, Jim Rodriguez, got the assignment and set about trying to create the artwork. In an attempt to capture a real life image of the cat, he gathered up his camera and went out in search of a mackerel tomcat. His search took him to several dumpsters found in the rear of restaurants. Unfortunately, this was at a time when an oriental restaurant, on route 25 in Long Island, was exposed in the Newsday newspaper for using cats in their cooking. Jim stopped off in the rear of a seafood restaurant in hopes of filming a feral tomcat, with no luck. However, a man emerged from the back asking what he was doing. Jim told him that he was looking for cats, which was apparently the *wrong* answer. The man angrily yelled out, "We ain't got no cats here," as Jim jumped in his car and took off.

He took a different course of action and visited the local animal shelter in Bay Shore. They didn't have any stripped cats, but he was informed that there was one running around their parking lot. He went out and immediately found a perfectly stripped young mackerel tabby. It wasn't long before the two became buddies and he photographed him from all angles. Based on the photos, he did several drawings showing the cat. Later, Dick Milligan, found a lion cub drawing in a dollar cartoon book and they decided to use this in place of the original request. They went with the posed artwork and added stripes to the cub to make it appear like a tomcat.

The 'Anytime Baby', motto was the idea of Norm Gandia, who came up with the slogan as a challenge to the U.S. Air Force F-15 Eagle. From those humble beginnings, a mascot was born!!

In the mid 70's, Officer Frank Gallagher, who worked out at the ESU School in Hanger #3 at Floyd Bennett Field, received a Tomcat decal from a friend of his who worked over at Grumman. Frank put it on his office door, not realizing what he had begun. A short time later, he saw the same logo now being used on Truck One.

In time, the decal would adorn other ESU trucks and the Tomcat logo and motto "Anytime, Baby..!" would become synonymous with the Emergency Service Unit.

Tomcat logo on Truck 1 (Photo courtesy of Tom Clemente / ClemcoGTI)

Tomcat logos on Truck 3 (Photo courtesy of Gerard Donnelly)

TRUCK PATCHES

In the 1980's, a new type of patch was introduced. These were referred to as *truck* patches and were produced as a sort of in-house item to promote a sense of *Esprit de Corps* among the members of ESU.

At that time, individual unit patches were somewhat of a novelty in the NYPD. In fact, there were only a handful of patches that were actually authorized by the NYPD for official wear.

So the introduction of these truck patches was quite unique, especially for collectors. However, by its very nature, it is not unusual that ESU would have been at the vanguard of this new wave. They had been a pioneer all along.

The foundation for this book is directly intertwined with these truck patches. Regrettably, it is also one of the areas which has proven to be a *minefield* for new collectors; seeking to obtain authentic ones from among the glut of reproductions that are still being offered.

TRUCK ONE (MANHATTAN)

The first Truck 1 patch, 'The Core of the Apple,' was created by Officer Frank Ferrara around 1991 and was produced by Stadri Emblem, when the company was based in Lower Manhattan.

During the design process, which was done with the input of Truck 1 members, several concepts were considered. Some were rejected and others were modified to be incorporated into what would later become the approved patch.

Below are a series of black and white concept art drawings that were submitted for member consideration and approval.

The first version featured the Tomcat, cradling a shotgun in one arm while leaning on the Twin Towers, inside an apple. The unit's lightning bolt logo appeared toward the bottom.

The second version removed the Tomcat and featured the unit's logo more prominently in the center, superimposed over a city skyline.

First two designs using an Apple motif (Artwork courtesy of Frank Ferrara.)

The third design incorporated the old blue truck in the center with the unit logo superimposed over the top. The fourth design added the Tomcat back along with a round border.

The only addition to this last design would be the ball-cap on the Tomcat. (*Artwork courtesy of Frank Ferrara.*)

The approved 5", fully embroidered round design featured the Tomcat, now wearing the ball cap, leaning on the unit's truck with a skyline inside an *'apple'* motif. The unit's logo, a large '1' with a lightning bolt, featured prominently in the center. There were two versions of the patch. The general issue one had a blue border design while the other had a silver Mylar border.

While the blue border was available to everyone, the Mylar version was limited to actual members of Truck 1. Many other trucks would follow suit, creating one patch to be given to those outside ESU and another for members of the unit. These would soon become known as a '*gang*' patches.

Because of the limited number of these produced, in contrast to the general issue one, they are some of the most coveted pieces among collectors.

On a historical note, the original '1 and lightning bolt' logo design, depicted on the patch, came about back in the 1980's, when several members of the unit wanted to have a large '1' made to affix to the front of the truck. As the story goes, Officer Frank LaSala had it made by a friend of his, but when they got it back, the metal '1' had a lightning bolt affixed to the back of it. The lightning bolt has been part of the unit's logo ever since.

Sadly, Officer LaSala was killed in the line of duty on January 10th, 1987, in a building fire several doors away from the Truck 1 quarters. When alerted to the fire, Officer LaSala donned a *SCOT* airpack and proceeded to the location where he rescued a number of residents before he became trapped.

While the logo no longer adorns the front of the truck, the original is still around, affixed to the Command Center door at the quarters of Truck 1.

Photo courtesy of Andy Bershard

In the late 1990's, a new 4.5", fully embroidered round patch was produced. It featured a more prominent skyline with the unit's logo in the center. Two gold stars were added to the border to memorialize the two officers from Truck 1 that had been killed in the line of duty: Frank LaSala and Officer Patrick O'Connor, who was killed on November 24th, 1971, when his ESU truck was struck by another vehicle on the Gowanus Expressway.

Interestingly enough, this new design is actually incorrect, as the lightning bolt design was flipped. It was probably done for aesthetics, but was inaccurate nonetheless.

The gang version of this design featured a grey thread border.

Truck 1 suffered another tragic loss during the attack on the World Trade Center on September 11th, 2001, when Police Officer Brian McDonnell was killed. After Officer McDonnell's death, the truck patch underwent another revision in 2002.

This time the patch the lightning bolt was repositioned to its proper direction. A new gold star was placed above the WTC buildings in memory of Officer McDonnell.

In 2003, Detective John McKenna from Truck 1 had another run of these patches produced. This version was done by Huntzman Enterprises and features their sticker on the reverse. A gang version, shown to the right, featuring gold Mylar stars and lightning bolt, was also produced.

Over the course of the next several years there would be additional gang versions produced.

In 2007, the second gang version featured a silver Mylar border. The third version, done in 2015, featured a silver Mylar '1' with a red Mylar border around it.

All three of these versions were done by Huntzman Enterprises and have the company's sticker on the reverse.

Below is artwork that was produced by Huntzman Enterprises in 2006 for two proposed designs. These were not adopted and no actual patches were ever produced.

TRUCK TWO (MANHATTAN)

The first Truck 2 patch 'Doing it 2 an Uptown Beat' is believed to have been produced back around 1991/92.

The 5", fully embroidered, round patch featured the unit's blue truck, the sign for the famous "Cotton Club" and the truck's mascot, a Boxer dog named Mojo, perched atop the Manhattanville Viaduct.

In 1999, a new 4", partially embroidered, round patch, 'Harlem', was produced by Officer Joe Vigiano of Truck 2. This version was designed by Vigiano's friend, David Smith, of Phoenix Sign and Design, who is a graphic designer from Caledonia, Michigan.

The first submitted design featured the Tomcat wearing a tuxedo and carrying an old school tommy gun. While it had all the key elements they were looking for, the legend "We Fly, You Die..." was deemed to be a *tad* bit politically incorrect.

The second graphic, removed the wording and swapped the positions of the Cotton Club logo and the number '2'.

Artwork courtesy of David Smith, **Phoenix Sign and Design**

Sadly, Detective Vigiano was one of the officers lost in the attack on September 11th, 2001.

In the history of the NYPD, Detective Vigiano is the only member of the department to be awarded the three highest medals: Medal of Honor, Combat Cross and Medal of Valor.

In 2014, Detective Brandon Watson of Truck 2 contacted Huntzman Enterprises to produce a new run of the 'Harlem' patch done by Detective Vigiano since the unit no longer had any.

In addition, a limited run of the original patch was also produced.

There were also gang versions done of both with Mylar lettering. The 'Doing it 2 an Uptown Beat' patch featured red Mylar lettering and the 'Harlem' patch featured blue Mylar lettering.

All of these patches feature the company's sticker on the reverse.

In 2014, Detective Watson also had a slightly smaller, fully embroidered, round patch produced by Huntzman Enterprises to be worn on the tactical vests.

This new design featured the same Tomcat design, done by Detective Vigiano, but in subdued colors.

This patch comes with a Velcro backing affixed to the rear.

TRUCK THREE (BRONX)

In 1993, Truck 3 released their first patch 'The Bronx'. This nearly 5" high, fully embroidered patch was designed by Officer Rick Martinez of the unit.

The design featured the unit's blue truck in the center, along with a large '3' positioned above it. Allegedly there were two prototypes that were produced before the unit selected the version shown below.

There was also a gang version of the patch produced as well and features a silver Mylar border.

Around 1994, a new, nearly 5", fully embroidered, oval patch debuted. This patch was also designed by Officer Martinez and it featured the unit's blue truck in the center, flanked by a large 'E' & '3'.

According to Officer Martinez there was no gang patch version of this design.

After one run the unit went back to using the original 'The Bronx' version.

In 1995, Officer Martinez produced a satirical 4.75" high, fully embroidered patch known as 'Anytime? Maybe'.

While not exactly a truck patch in the truest sense; this patch was more of an inside joke. The design featured a Tomcat, sleeping on a bed, surrounded by several bullet holes and the legend 'Is that confirmed, Central?'

In 1999, Sergeant Brian Wall designed the 'Anytime, in the Bronx....!' Patch. This design was based in part on the patch that Detective Joe Vigiano had done for Truck 7. The 4.5" high, fully embroidered insignia was produced by KB Emblem and features the company's sticker on the reverse of this patch.

The design featured a Tomcat holding a 'Y' bar, which was used to control emotionally disturbed persons (EDP's), in one hand and a shotgun in the other, leaning on a green '3'.

There was no gang version of this patch produced.

This style remained in use until 2001, when the design underwent a change to memorialize the three members of Truck 3 who were killed in the line of duty on September 11th, 2001.

Originally, the three gold colored stars were meant to signify Truck 3. Now the three stars represented the three members who had died in the line of duty. The stars now included the initials for Officer Vincent Danz (VD), Officer Jerome Dominguez (JD), and Officer Walter Weaver (WW).

This 4.5", fully embroidered design was done by Detective Dave Brink and again produced by KB Emblem.

In 2004, Detective Brink teamed up with Huntzman Enterprises to produce a new unit patch that commemorated the 75th Anniversary of Emergency Service Unit.

The new design incorporated some of the previous patch elements, but was in a larger, 5" round size. The new fully embroidered design had the Tomcat leaning on a diamond with the '3' inside of it and the anniversary dates '1930' and '2005' on the outer border.

A gang version, featuring gold Mylar dates, was also produced. Both designs feature the company's sticker on the reverse.

In 2009, Detective Tom Murphy commissioned Huntzman Enterprises to produce an updated version of the Truck 3 patch.

Originally, two prototype graphics were produced for consideration, one with a blue border and the other a green.

The same 4.5" size was used, but the Tomcat was enlarged and was now outfitted with a 9mm pistol along with an M-4 rifle. The stars were also repositioned.

The truck chose the green bordered, fully embroidered design and the only other change was the addition of the initials in the stars of the Truck 3 officers killed in the line of duty.

There was also a gang version of the patch produced with a silver Mylar border. Both versions feature the company's sticker on the back.

This new design was even featured in the 2009, Truck 3 Christmas card, with the Tomcat being appropriately decked out with a Santa hat and an ornament hanging from the barrel of the M-4.

While not a truck patch, per se, in 2014, Detective Roger Savage produced a subdued, partially embroidered patch for Truck 3 that is worn on the bicep protector on the heavy vest.

The rectangular design features a gray number '3' in the centers surrounded by the three stars and is affixed to the vest by Velcro.

TRUCK FOUR (BRONX)

The first Truck 4 patch 'Ice Station Zebra' was produced around 1995, by Officer David Smith of Truck 4. The original artwork was produced by Officer Kevin Clark, of the 44 Precinct, whom Smith had previously worked with.

The 4.5" round, partially embroidered design featured an ESU truck, falling through a hole in the ice, and their quarters depicted as an igloo.

Pictured below, on the left, is the original artwork, created by Officer Clark, from which the patch was produced.

Artwork courtesy of David Smith, ESU Retired

The second patch, 'Bronx Zoo', was produced sometime prior to 2001. The nearly 4", fully embroidered, round patch featured the unit's truck with the old Yankee Stadium in the background.

Contrary to what many collectors think, the flags atop the stadium do not indicate the years that the Yankee's had won the World Series, but instead denote the NYPD precincts that Truck 4 covers.

In 2001, the patch underwent a modest redesign. The overall size was increased to 4.5" and the word 'Zoo' removed. This version was produced by KB Emblem and features their sticker on the reverse.

In 2003, Detective Evan Schwerner had Huntzman Enterprises produce the unit's new patch.

The overall size of the fully embroidered patch was enlarged to 5" and the old blue truck was replaced by one with the new white paint scheme. The size of Yankee Stadium was also increased.

This patch features the company's sticker on the reverse. There was no gang version of this patch produced.

In 2014, Detective Kris Cataldo had Huntzman Enterprises produce the unit's new patch.

The overall design elements of the 5", fully embroidered patch remained largely the same as the preceding design, but the old Yankee Stadium was removed and replaced with the façade of the new stadium.

In addition, two gold stars were added to the top with the initials of the two Truck 4 members who were killed in the 9/11 attack – Sgt. John Coughlin (JC) and Police Officer Stephen Driscoll (SD).

This patch features the company's sticker on the reverse. There was a limited run gang version of this patch produced with silver Mylar lettering and gold Mylar stars.

TRUCK FIVE (STATEN ISLAND)

The first Truck 5 patch was designed and produced in 1990, by Officer's Brian Hearn and Ed Trentacosta.

The 4.25", partially embroidered, diagonal design has a knife cut border and is in the shape of Staten Island. It has a large '5' in the center surrounded by a Hurst tool, dive flag and a medical symbol.

According to Officer Hearn, the patch was produced locally on Staten Island and was an extremely limited run, numbering only in the *teens*.

In 1993, after the first attack on the World Trade Center, Officer Hearn designed a new, 5.25", fully embroidered, shield shaped patch which he envisioned as being a potential prototype for all ESU trucks at large scene responses.

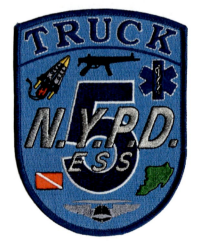

This new design featured a large '5' with the lettering Truck on top and NYPD ESS in the center. It also incorporated various symbols of ESU capabilities: Hurst tool, medical symbol, dive flag, helicopter and MP5 submachine gun.

The idea was that the '5' could be replaced with any Truck number. This patch was also produced locally by another officer who also owned a police equipment store in Staten Island.

In 2005, Detective Dave Smutek redesigned the Truck 5 patch. The new 4.5", fully embroidered, round patch featured the unit's new white truck in the center next to the Verrazano-Narrows Bridge.

It was produced by Mainly Monograms in West Nyack, N.Y.

In 2014, Officer Nick Gentile, along with input from members of the unit, designed a new patch featuring the unit's new Mack - Saulsbury truck.

While the patch maintained all the key design elements from the previous one, this version has the distinction of being the first woven ESU patch. Pictured below, on the left, is the original artwork for the patch.

Artwork courtesy of Anthony Lisi

Woven patches use thinner thread and are stitched in a continuous design. This allows for finer detail in both the design and text of the patch. Since the patch is woven, it has a smooth appearance with no raised texture.

The patch was produced locally on Staten Island.

TRUCK SIX (BROOKLYN)

Around 1986, Officer Bob Gardella of Truck 6 produced the unit's first patch, the infamous 'Ram's Head' design. The artwork was done by Gardella's wife, Susan, based on input from the members of the truck.

My research indicates that this is probably the very first truck patch produced by ESU.

The original intent was to depict a black sheep because at the time Truck 6 was known as the 'black sheep' truck in certain quarters; a name and reputation worn like a badge of honor. Unfortunately, the black sheep came out looking more like a ram's head and the name stuck.

This partially embroidered, shield shaped patch was produced in a very limited run by a company located in the West Village section of Manhattan.

Around 1989/90 the patch was redesigned by Officer's Tony Cuccia, Pat Murphy (son of former Police Commissioner Patrick V. Murphy) and Jimmy Cole.

The new 5", fully embroidered design included the Verrazano-Narrows Bridge and the Coney Island Parachute Drop in the background with the unit's blue truck positioned in the middle.

This patch design was later made into a painting by Officer Tom DeFresco, of the 62 Pct., whose brother, Rick DeFresco worked in Truck 6. The painting is still on display in the trucks quarters.

Photo courtesy of Pete Whalen

Sometime in the early 90's, the patch underwent some minor revisions, including the addition of a '6' on the front grill. The size was also reduced to 4.5"

In 2003, Detective Pete Whalen, with the help of his brother Tom Whalen and Ed Vandenberg, both of Truck 6, redesigned the patch.

The size remained the same, but they replaced the old blue truck with the new white one.

This patch was produced by KB Emblems and has the company's sticker on the back.

In 2007, Detective Whalen contracted with Huntzman Enterprises to produce a new run of the patches.

The overall design remained the same, but the truck was made slightly larger and a yellow '6' was put on the front grill.

There was a regular version with blue border as well as a gang version with a silver Mylar border.

In addition, there was an initial run that was produced in error. This version, with a blue border, featured a truck with silver Mylar windows, side mirror and bumper.

All three versions have the company's sticker on the reverse.

The Infamous 'Duck' Patch

Anyone familiar with the history of New York City can probably tell you about the 'sibling rivalry' that exists between members of the NYPD and the FDNY. This is especially true for those members of ESU, who often find themselves responding to rescue calls at the same time as FDNY.

It was inevitable that this would one day spill over into the insignia world, to be forever immortalized in cloth. This particular design, a 4", partially embroidered patch, is attributed only to a *'former member'* of Truck 6, and was produced back in the 90's.

The legend says it all: *"When only the Finest will do – Call ESU."*

TRUCK SEVEN (BROOKLYN)

In 1989, Detective Dave Brink designed and produced the very first Truck 7 patch.

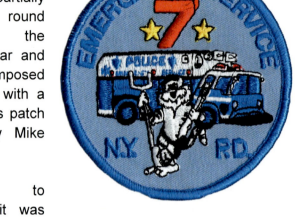

The 4", partially embroidered, round design featured the Tomcat with 'Y' bar and shotgun, superimposed over a blue truck with a red '7' on top. This patch was produced by Mike Asher.

According to Detective Brink, it was subsequently discovered years later that a second design, featuring Mylar detailing, had also been produced by Asher, but it was not an approved version.

In 1997, the late Detective Joe Vigiano teamed up with his graphic artist friend, David Smith, in order to design a new patch for Truck 7.

Detective Vigiano wanted something that more closely reflected the design of the original Navy Tomcat patch. The result was a 4.5", partially embroidered patch that featured the Tomcat, cradling a shotgun, while leaning against a large, red '7'. On the bottom tab was the legend 'Feelin' Lucky...?'

On each side of the border was a pair of dice with the numbers '5' and '2' to signify Truck 7.

UNCOMMON VALOR

Original letter from 1997, by Detective Vigiano to David Smith, outlining his ideas for the Truck 7 patch.

> Dave,
>
> The pictures we took did not come out so we dug out this photo.
>
> The logo is the Grumman "Any Time Baby" Cat holding a shotgun.
>
> Also maybe on the back. Something like
>
> Lucky Seven
>
> 🎲🎲
>
> or something better
>
> Give me a call if you need more. or dimensions
>
> Joe Vig
>
> I'm going to Florida 1/25 2/5 so call me after   Vig

(*Courtesy of David Smith, Phoenix Sign & Graphic*)

Pictured below, on the left, is the original artwork, created by David Smith, from which the patch was produced.

The second version of this design maintained all the key elements of the first version, but changed the numbering on the dice to '4' and '3'.

This 2nd version was produced sometime in late 1997.

As the story goes, there was a shooting involving members of Truck 7 and a local newspaper ran a headline reading: 'Guess he wasn't lucky.' The Police Commissioner, at that time, did not like the inference, so this led to Detective Vigiano re-designing the patch in 1998.

On a historical note, the 'Feelin' Lucky…?' patch was the first to accurately portray the Tomcat with his two tails. The reason for the two tails goes back to the F-14 which was a 'twin tail' aircraft. The use of the twin tails on the Truck 7 patches remains in use today.

In the updated design, he removed the words 'Feelin' Lucky...' and replaced it with 'Brooklyn. The dice were also changed back to the original '5' and '2'.

Pictured below, on the left, is the original artwork, created by Smith, from which the patch was produced.

In 2002, after the attack of September 11th, a new memorial patch was designed.

Elements of the previous design were incorporated into a new 4.5", partially embroidered patch that featured a grey silhouette of the NYC skyline, with the Twin Towers in the background, superimposed over a waving American flag.

On this design, the dice were also changed back to '4' and '3'.

Two yellow stars were also added to memorialize the two Truck 7 officers who were killed: Officer Ronald Kloepfer and Officer Santos Valentin.

This patch was produced by Star Emblem.

In 2008, Detective Al Gut had Huntzman Enterprises design a new patch.

This new 4.5", fully embroidered design updated the previous one done by Detective Vigiano and now incorporated three memorial stars. Two white stars represented Officer's Kloepfer and Valentin, while a yellow star memorialized Sergeant Keith Ferguson, who died on January 31st, 2004, while in pursuit of a suspect.

There was also a gang patch produced which features gold and silver Mylar stars and gold lettering NYPD. Both designs have the company's sticker on the back.

TRUCK EIGHT (BROOKLYN)

The first Truck 8 patch was designed back in the late 1980's.

The 3.5", partially embroidered, round patch featured only four colors in total. In the center was the Williamsburg Bridge with a small, light blue truck at the bottom.

In the early 1990's, the design was updated.

The new 3.5" patch retained all the key elements of the original patch, but was now fully embroidered and featured a larger blue truck at the bottom.

Around 2002/03, the Truck 8 patch design was changed. The new 3.25", fully embroidered patch, was designed by Detective Matt Sproul. This design was now in the shape of the regulation ESU insignia.

The first version featured an American flag design in the background, with the legend 'The Flagship' and an angry looking '8-Ball' in the center, chomping on a lightning bolt.

A second, 3.25" design, also done by Detective Sproul, had the NYPD flag colors in the background and in the top arc the lettering 'Truck 8'.

In 2005, the design was once again updated, this time based on a painting at Truck 8 quarters that was done by retired officer Frank Garafolo.

This new 4" fully embroidered, round patch was produced by Detective James Piccolo and features the Tomcat leaning on an 8-Ball.

The design also includes three stars, memorializing the three Truck 8 officers who were killed in the line of duty. One star is for Sergeant Rodney Gillis, who was killed in the terror attack on September 11th, 2001. The other two stars are for Patrolmen Stephen Gilroy and Salvatore Spinola.

Ptl. Gilroy was killed on January 19th, 1973 at the infamous 'Al's Sporting Goods' robbery. Due to the quick response of officers, the perpetrators were prevented from leaving, but this resulted in a hostage situation developing. Unfortunately, the perpetrators inside the location also had unlimited access to rifles, shotgun and ammunition. Ptl. Gilroy, who was one of the first ESU officers on the scene, was killed when shots rang out from inside the location.

On October 2nd, 1969, Ptl. Spinola and his partner responded to a radio run for a Department of Water Supply, Gas and Electric worker down in a manhole. Ptl. Spinola donned a gas filter mask and descended into the manhole. Unfortunately, the gas had displaced the oxygen and Ptl. Spinola was overcome. He was pulled from the manhole and rushed to the hospital where he died.

TRUCK NINE (QUEENS)

In 1995, Officer Mike Laxton designed the first Truck 9 patch.

The 4.5", partially embroidered, round design featured the unit's blue truck superimposed over the JFK Airport, Air Traffic Control Tower. The two planes depicted on the patch were supposed to represent Air Force One and the Concorde.

Over the course of the next few years the design would undergo two different changes. The first was the repositioning of the truck, which now faced to the left of the patch.

The third change was a minor one, adding a 'white wall' tire to the front wheel.

In 2003, Detective's Andrew Bershad and Todd Sessa redesigned the patch.

The new 4", fully embroidered, round patch was designed with the intent to distance themselves from the JFK airport theme.

The new design featured the Tomcat holding an M-4 rifle and leaning against the number '9'. In the background was the unit's new white truck.

This design was produced by Silkraft in Patchogue, Long Island.

TRUCK TEN (QUEENS)

In 1988, Officer's Glenn Klein and Rich Hackford designed and produced the first Truck 10 patch.

The 3", partially embroidered, round design featured the World's Fair *Unisphere* in the center, with the bomb robot, which Truck 10 maintained, superimposed over the *Unisphere,* along with the 'jaws of life' Hurst tool at the bottom. It was produced by a company in lower Manhattan

Around 1991/92, Officer's Glenn Klein and Tom Langone designed and produced a new Truck 10 patch. The size of this partially embroidered round design was increased to 4.25" and featured an improved *Unisphere* in the background along with the unit's large blue truck in the foreground. It had a dark blue border.

Around 1993, after the blue patches ran out, Officer's Klein and Langone redesigned the Truck 10 patch. This patch maintained all the elements of the previous design, but now featured a red border and was reduced to 4" in size.

Around 1995, Officer's Klein and Langone designed and produced a new Truck 10 patch.

This 4" patch maintained all the elements of the previous design, but now featured a silver Mylar border.

In 2002, after the September 11th attack, Detective Vinny Manco designed a 4" memorial patch to honor the two members of Truck 10 that had been killed in the attack.

The new 4", partially embroidered, round patch featured a white truck, superimposed over a black skyline featuring the Twin Towers, with a flag background. The names Paul Talty and Thomas Langone are written on the borders, along with Emergency Truck 10 and the date: Sept 11th, 2001, in a banner below. It is believed to have been produced by Star Emblem.

In 2002, several members of the unit, including Sergeant Paul Hargrove and Detective's Tom Bourne, Steven Stefanakos and Jim McCormick, designed a new memorial patch.

This 4", fully embroidered, round patch was a redesign of the older issue patch. It now featured the unit's white truck superimposed over the *Unisphere* with the initials PT and TL along the border. It was produced by Colorfully Yours in Deer Park, Long Island.

In 2011, Detective Rob Isernia had Huntzman Enterprises produce an updated version of the prior design.

The new 4", fully embroidered design featured a more accurate *Unisphere* in the center along with the white truck.

There was also a gang patch produced which featured a silver Mylar border. Both designs have the manufacturer's sticker on the back.

In 2014, Detective Rob Isernia once again had Huntzman Enterprises produce an updated version of the prior design.

The new 4", fully embroidered patch featured the unit's new Mack - Saulsbury truck in the center. This design has the manufacturer's sticker on the back.

OTHER UNITS

APPREHENSION TACTICAL TEAM (A-TEAM) / CAT

The first Apprehension Tactical Team (A-Team) patch debuted in the 1990's.

The first issue was a 3.5", partially embroidered, round patch that featured two ESU officers performing a tactical entry in the center.

Subsequently there were two additional designs produced.

One was a 3.5", partially embroidered patch, kept the design elements of the original, but updated the detailing of the two officers. The second, partially embroidered design increased the size to 4" and was done in a subdued color scheme.

In 2008, Detective Tom Longa designed the 4th issue patch for the unit. The 4.25", fully embroidered, shield shaped patch, features a kneeling ESU officer, superimposed over the NYPD logo. It has a Velcro backing.

In 2012, Detective Longa had Huntzman Enterprises produce the unit's 5th patch. The 4.5", fully embroidered, shield shaped featured a gladiator's helmet in the center with the legend *Cohors Praetoria* (Praetorian Guard), around the helmet, and the Roman numerals VII / IV.

There was a gang version done with silver Mylar lettering and numerals. Both versions feature a Velcro backing.

In 2014, Detective Tom Longa had Huntzman Enterprises produce the 6th issue design for the unit. The 4.5", fully embroidered, shield shaped patch retained all the key elements of the previous design, but the lettering *Cohors Praetoria* was repositioned and the date 1989 added.

There was a gang version done with silver Mylar lettering and numerals. Both versions feature a Velcro backing.

COUNTER ASSAULT TEAM

In 1998, Detective Dave Brink designed a 3.5", fully embroidered, round patch for the Counter Assault Team. It was produced by KB Emblem.

The numbers in the banner indicated the trucks that had CAT vehicles assigned to them: 1, 3, 7, & 10.

COUNTER SNIPER TEAM

In 1998, Officer Rick Martinez designed the two original, 3.5", fully embroidered patches for the Counter Sniper Team.

The first design was in the shape of the standard ESU patch and featured the WTC skyline inside a sniper scope reticle. The top of the patch bore the legend *'Concorde'* which was the team's call-sign.

The second design elements were the same, but the call-sign was removed and the lettering was changed. The top of the patch now said 'NYPD ESU' and 'Long Range'.

After the September 11th attack, the patch was modified slightly. In 2002, Officer Martinez re-designed the 3rd issue patch for the Counter Sniper Team.

The skyline was changed to a silver Mylar and the date 9-11-01 and number '23', signifying the number of NYPD officers killed in the attack, was added.

Around 2002/03, Detective Matt Sproul slightly modified the CST patch. The design elements were the same as the 2nd issue, but the colors were now changed.

One version featured a subdued green motif, while the other version a subdued gray design.

HAMMER / WMD

After the September 11th attack, and in response to letters being sent that contained Anthrax, a new unit, the **HA**zardous **M**aterial **M**itigation **E**mergency **R**esponse team, was created to deal with the subsequent threats posed.

In 2001, Detective Dave Brink created the nearly 4" wide, fully embroidered, HAMMER team patch and it was produced by KB Emblem.

In 2008, Detective Dan Condon had Huntzman Enterprises design the original Weapons of Mass Destruction Team patch. The 4", fully embroidered, round patch featured an ESU patch and Grim Reaper with a grey skyline underneath them. It had various images relating to Chemical, Biological, Radiological, Nuclear and Explosives. It has the company's sticker on the back.

A subdued version of the patch was also produced.

In 2009, Detective Condon had Huntzman Enterprises re-design the Weapons of Mass Destruction Team patch.

The 2nd issue maintained the size and most of the design elements from the first issue patch, but changed some of the placards and positioning for the Chemical, Biological, Radiological, Nuclear and Explosives images. It has the company's sticker on the back.

A subdued version of the patch was also produced.

In 2010, Detective Patrick Barry had Huntzman Enterprises re-design the Weapons of Mass Destruction Team patch. It has the company's sticker on the back.

The 3rd issue patch was completely redesigned. The new 4.25", fully embroidered patch now featured the Tomcat in the center, leaning on a bio-hazard placard and holding a gas mask.

The unit name was also changed to WMD Response Team and on the bottom tab was the legend 'Any WMD's, Baby...?'

A subdued version of the patch was also produced.

EMERGENCY MEDICAL SQUAD

In 2004, Officer Steve Tomasulo had Huntzman Enterprises design Emergency Medical Squad patch.

The 3.5", fully embroidered, ESU shaped patch featured a blue star of life emblem in the center along with a medical caduceus. It has the company's sticker on the back.

A gold Mylar bordered gang patch was also produced.

TACTICAL MEDIC

In 2003, Detective John Busching, of Truck 7, designed the original Tactical Medic patch when the unit was first established.

The 3.5", partially embroidered, ESU shaped patch featured a blue star of life emblem in the center along with crossed spears and a sword, along with a yellow cardiac rhythm reading in the background.

The patch was intended to be worn on the medic's backpack as well as the heavy vest.

On September 11th, 2001, Officer John Busching responded to the attack on the World Trade Center. During the search, he located Port Authority Police Officer John McLoughlin. Busching administered life-saving medical treatment to Officer McLoughlin for twelve hours while rescue teams worked to dig him out by hand. Officer McLoughlin would be the last person pulled out of Ground Zero alive and this rescue would be the basis for Oliver Stone's film: *World Trade Center*.

During the course of my research I was advised that an updated color version was produced several years later. This design reportedly kept all the main design elements of the original, but removed the yellow cardiac rhythm sign from the back.

While I am still trying to confirm the details on this patch, the photo below shows the decal version of this insignia being worn on the ESU construction hard hat.

Photo Courtesy of Andy Bershard

Around 2006/07, the Tactical Medic patch was redesigned. For safety concerns, the officers wanted a subdued version, which didn't stand out as much as the color version.

A roughly 3", partially embroidered patch was produced and has a Velcro backing which allows it to be affixed to the vest or gear.

CANINE

One of the most difficult areas to research are the patches of the ESU K9 unit. Principally, this is due to the fact that the patches are not authorized for wear, except on baseball hats.

For so many years the patches were private purchases, meaning that a K9 officer could purchase a patch at a local police shop and wear it on his hat.

The first recorded use of a K9 patch was back in the early 1980's. It was, however, very short lived. By most accounts the actual time it was used was in the sixty day mark. According to information that has been passed down, the unit was considered too small to have their own patch and it was ordered to be removed.

The roughly 4.25", fully embroidered, triangular design was styled after the Mounted patch and featured a German Shepherd dog in the center.

Many years ago I had a photo showing the patch in use. Unfortunately, several hard drives later, the photo is lost to history.

The next patch came out about a decade later, in the early 1990's and was followed up a short time later by another version. Both patches were approximately 3.25", conforming to the size of the standard ESU patch and were partially embroidered.

The first patch featured the lettering 'K-9 Unit' and the next version said 'NYPD K-9 Unit'. Unlike the triangle patch, these were intended for wear on ball caps.

Currently there are two authorized ball caps for K-9. One features direct embroidery and the other is a partially embroidered patch shown below.

In addition to the regular ESU patches that the K-9 officers wear on the left sleeve of their BDU's they wear other unit insignia. I have opted to include this insignia here, as it is specific to their K-9 assignment.

On the collar of the BDU's they wear small tabs, like the ones that say ESU, except these say K9. Additionally, they also wear 4"wide, partially embroidered, rectangular breast patches, like those shown below.

Like the other BDU patches described earlier, since these are all private purchases from various manufacturers, it is not uncommon to encounter minor differences in both size and coloring.

On the back of the BDU's is a 9", partially embroidered patch.

Over the years I have also obtained several other K-9 patches which are purported to be from the ESU K-9. However, since these patches exceed the size used on hats, I am unsure if they were ever actually used by the unit or simply produced for collectors. I will continue to research them for possible inclusion in a later addition.

FEMA NYTF-1

In 1995, after the terrorist attack at the Alfred P. Murrah Federal Building in Oklahoma City, Officer Rick Martinez designed the original Urban Search and Rescue patch for the FEMA NYTF-1, which ESU is a part of, so that members responding would have their own identifiable insignia.

The large 4.5", fully embroidered, shield shaped design features the familiar NYC skyline on the top, with the Twin Towers, and has the legend: 'FEMA NY-TF1 New York City Urban Search and Rescue Task Force'. The border features gold Mylar lettering.

EVENTS & MISCELLANEOUS

EVENTS & MISCELLANEOUS

Over the years, there have been several patches produced by various ESU units to commemorate specific events. Below, listed in chronological order, are a number of different ones. Where possible, I have listed who produced them and for what reason.

While not an attributable ESU patch, *per se*, I don't think you could exclude the patch that launched the rest. It was not long after the Tomcat decal first began to appear on the sides of the trucks, that the patch was co-opted for use by members of ESU.

There are any number of versions and variations that were used, but this one would serve as the foundation for the future appearances of the Tomcat.

The next generation of the 'Anytime, Baby....!" patch saw the Navy Tomcat fully transformed into his ESU alter-ego.

This 4", partially embroidered, round patch featured the traditional Tomcat, who now sported a ball cap, clutching a 'Y' bar in one hand and cradled a shotgun in the other.

In the 1980's, an entire series of *'Big Apple'* patches came out. They were all the same 4.5", partially embroidered design, that featured a police officer's shield in the center, but where the numbers would normally be was the name of a specific command.

I have limited the September 11th memorial patches to only those that have a direct link to ESU, either specifically created or utilized by members of ESU. The reason for this is that there were so many unsolicited 'memorial' patches, created after the attack, that were done simply to cash-in on the tragedy and line the pockets of various manufacturers. I don't believe they should be included here, simply because they refer to ESU.

After 9/11, a 3.5", partially embroidered, memorial patch was produced by a member of ESU honoring the 23 officers lost in the attack.

The ESU style patch featured a purple line drawn through the center of the ESU truck with the number '23' in the center and 9/11 underneath.

In 2001, the Mount Vernon, NY Police, Emergency Service Unit produced a 3.25" wide, partially embroidered, rectangular memorial patch.

While not an NYPD ESU patch, I include this design because I know of at least one member of ESU who actually wore this patch on his uniform jacket. To me, an actual worn patch has more credibility.

In 2002, retired Officer George Olivero, who retired from Truck 7 just prior to 9/11, had Detective Dave Brink assist him in designing a 9/11 ESU motorcycle ride memorial patch.

The large, 5.25" wide, partially embroidered, rectangular patch featured the numbers '911' in a red, white and blue motif, with the '1's forming the twin towers. In each of the towers were the names of each member from ESU who was killed on 9/11. The patch was produced by KB Emblem.

In 2002, Detective Matt Sproul designed a 3.5", fully embroidered, detective shield shaped patch.

The badge patch featured the ESU truck in the center and the letters 'ESU' inside the number panel.

In 2002, Detective Dave Brink had Huntzman Enterprises design a 4", fully embroidered, round patch to commemorate the 2004 Republican National Convention, which was hosted by New York City.

The design featured the NYC skyline with both the NYPD and ESU patches flanking the RNC logo.

The patch has the company's sticker affixed to the back.

In 2005, Detective Sean Mulcahy had Huntzman Enterprises design a 4.5", fully embroidered patch to commemorate the 75th anniversary of ESU.

The design featured a Tomcat in an old ¾ length reefer coat, carrying a tommy-gun and leaning on an ESU patch. The background was the NYPD flag. Around the inner border were '25' gold Mylar stars representing each of the ESU officers who had been killed in the line of duty at that time.

Additionally, the dates '1930-2005', along with the buttons on the Tomcat's reefer coat, and '75th' were all done in gold Mylar.

The patch has the company's sticker affixed to the back.

In 2002, Detective Sean Mulcahy had Huntzman Enterprises design a 4.5", fully embroidered, round patch to commemorate the 'past & present' of ESU.

The design featured two Tomcats. One wore an old ¾ length reefer coat, and carried a tommy-gun, while the other wore a modern tactical vest and carried an M-4. Both Tomcats leaned on an ESU patch. The background was the NYC skyline and the American flag.

The patch has the company's sticker affixed to the back.

In 2007, Detective Sean Mulcahy had Huntzman Enterprises design a 4", fully embroidered, round patch to commemorate St. Patrick's Day.

The design featured an ESU patch held in place by two lions and a knight's helmet above. The ESU patch featured a green truck, an *homage* to the 1930's Mack truck, and along the border was a yellow and white Celtic knot.

The patch has the company's sticker affixed to the back.

In 2008, Detective Dave Brink had Huntzman Enterprises design a 4", fully embroidered, round patch to commemorate April 2008 visit of Pope Benedict XVI.

The design featured an ESU patch with Pope Benedict's seal, superimposed over the yellow and white Papal flag.

Along the border were listed the venues that Pope Benedict was appearing at: St. Patrick's Cathedral, Ground Zero, Yankee Stadium & the United Nations.

The patch has the company's sticker affixed to the back.

In 2009, Detective Sean Mulcahy had Huntzman Enterprises design a 4.25", fully embroidered, round patch to honor the retired members of ESU.

The design featured a Tomcat, wearing a pair of Oakley sunglasses, a Panama hat, Hawaiian shirt, smoking a cigar and holding a Pina Colada.

In the background was a tropical sunset, a surfboard and a shark's fin in the background. On the bottom was the legend 'Retired, Baby....!'

The patch has the company's sticker affixed to the back.

In 2011, as part of their annual St. Patrick's Day line, Huntzman Enterprises produced a commemorative patch.

The 4.5", fully embroidered design featured a modified ESU patch in the center, superimposed over an Irish and NYPD flag. The ESU patch featured a green truck. Along the border was the lettering St. Patrick's Day – New York City and the date: 2011.

The patch was a limited run of 100 pieces. It has the company's sticker affixed to the back along with an individual number.

In 2012, after getting requests from members of ESU, Huntzman Enterprises produced an ESU themed patch based on their 2011 St. Patrick's Day commemorative patch.

The 4.5", fully embroidered design featured an ESU patch superimposed over an American and NYPD flag. There were two different designs. On the first the ESU patch featured a green truck and on the second it featured the traditional blue truck.

The patch has the company's sticker affixed to the back.

THE JOHN D'ALLARA BSA PATCH

In 2004, a series of three Boy Scout patches were designed by Todd Lamison for the Patriots' Path Council, Fishawack District, NJ to honor the memory of Officer John D'Allara of Truck 2.

Officer D'Allara and his brother had been involved in Scouting when they were younger and it had left a lasting impact on Officer D'Allara. He even accredited his time in the Boy Scout's for his decision to go into law enforcement.

After his death on 9/11, his friend Dean Hoffman, approached Todd Lamison with the idea of designing a service achievement patch to honor John and his commitment to Scouting.

Todd designed the patch in cooperation with John's wife, Carol, his brother, Daniel, and Dean Hoffman. The end result was a 4", fully embroidered patch that recognized John and his love of climbing.

On the top was the lettering 'John D'Allara' and at the bottom was 'NYPD'. The patch featured two Scouts climbing in the foreground and the NYC skyline in the background. A red 'fleur de lis', representing the BSA logo, is in the center. In the final version, the date: 9/11/01 is 'ghosted out', using black on black thread.

The patch was produced by Sunshine Emblem.

There were three different versions produced. One featured a blue border, one a silver Mylar border, and another with a gold Mylar border. One version of the patch was first awarded in 2006, during a climb-a-thon event. Another version could be earned for completing a series of service oriented tasks.

While not an ESU patch, *per se*, this insignia serves to keep Officer D'Allara's memory alive through an organization he was proudly associated with and, in the spirit of this book, I feel it deserves to be included here.

Original artwork courtesy of Todd Lamison

For more information on the service award please visit the Patriot's Path Council website:

http://fishawack.ppbsa.org/Dallara/JD%20Award.htm

NYC HOUSING POLICE - ERU

On October 8th, 1993, the NYC Housing Authority Police, Emergency Rescue Unit rolled out into history. The unit would survive as an independent entity for only 10 short months when it was merged into the NYPD ESU on August 15th, 1994, during what has been colloquially referred to as the 'Hostile Takeover'.

It was the last of the big four city agencies to have its own emergency response unit. Previously, elevator jobs and EDP's were handled by NYPD's ESU which added to the inter-agency rivalry that existed.

At the time of its creation the unit consisted of 43 members: 1 captain, 1 lieutenant, 6 sergeants, 2 detectives and 33 police officers. Three of those original members, Sergeant John Coughlin, Sergeant Karl Smith and P.O. Vincent Danz, would later be lost during the attacks of September 11th, 2001.

There were only 4 REP's (small trucks) and two RMP's for the supervisors to cover all 5 boroughs.

The ERU was stationed in the basement of the Ravenswood Houses in Queens.

The Trucks went by the call signs R1, R2 R3 & R4. Each truck was staffed by three officers at all times.

On paper, R1 would handle PSA 1, 2 and 3 (Brooklyn), R2, would handle PSA 4, 5 and 6 (Manhattan), R3 would handle PSA

7, 8, and 9 (Bronx & Queens) and R4 was a back-up. However, in reality, whoever was closest to the job would handle the call.

Prior to its official start in October 1993, several insignia designs were produced.

The first design was done by Officer Charles Rubin. It was circular in shape with the lettering 'New York City' on top and 'Housing Police' on the bottom. In the center was the NYC skyline and inside a rectangular box were the words 'Emergency Rescue'.

Initially this design was produced as a silk screen image for work tee shirts. The front logo was in full color and the reverse had the words 'Housing / Rescue / Police' emblazoned on the back in large letters. Later, the image was also used to create collar brass. When this was done, the medical caduceus was omitted from the design.

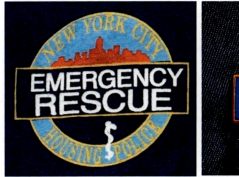 

Photo's courtesy of Kristie Maryou.

Later, the design was given to Sergeant Brian Wall's wife, who redesigned it into a large, oval shaped design, with input from the other members.

There were three prototypes that were produced, prior to the selected official patch. The first design was 6" high and fully embroidered. It featured a silver gray skyline with the lettering 'NYC Housing Police Department / Emergency Rescue Service'.

The star of life was red and had a black caduceus. This style was rejected for the size and wrong colors.

The 2nd prototype was roughly 5" high and fully embroidered. The coloring in the caduceus was corrected, but this time it featured a dark gray skyline that made the skyline difficult to see. This version was also rejected.

The 3rd prototype was a dramatic departure in terms of coloring and lettering placement. The 5", fully embroidered patch is almost identical to the approved version, except that the Twin Towers are placed directly under the letter 'H' and somewhat obscured.

The official patch was selected and was issued to the members in late September 1993, just days before the unit was officially activated. It is almost identical to the 3rd prototype with the exception that the Twin Towers were moved to the right slightly and now the skyline included both the Empire State Building as well as the Chrysler Building.

These patches were worn on the right shirt sleeve along with the collar brass pictured above.

Series of 3rd Issue prototype graphics (Courtesy of Brian Wall)

In the course of my research, I became aware that during the time the unit was designing their insignia, another design had been submitted to the HAPD. This large design depicted a cop rappelling down on it. The unit did not like the proposed design and actually went ahead with procuring their own patches. It is unknown what happened to this artwork.

In addition, the nylon duty jackets also had lettering directly embroidered to the reverse, which read: 'Housing Police Emergency Rescue Service'.

Photo courtesy of Kristie Maryou.

There were also two different style baseball caps that were used. The first style just had the lettering 'Housing Police' directly embroidered in the front.

Photo courtesy of Kristie Maryou.

The 2nd issue baseball hat actually had the unit's patch direct embroidered on the front.

This direct embroidered logo (on the left) is compared below next to an actual 3", fully embroidered, hat size patch which surfaced in 1994.

It is unsure whether this patch was a later issued item or was just produced and offered by police equipment shops in New York City. Officially, at least as of this writing, the direct embroidered version was the only approved one.

In addition to the hat patches there was also a decal that was worn, affixed to the blue construction helmets the unit used. These decals are the same design as the shoulder patch and were also used, albeit in a much larger format, on the unit trucks (see vehicle photo below).

Photo courtesy of Kristie Maryou.

An interesting side note on the truck decals. Originally, the ERS decal was supposed to be displayed on both sides of the truck, and on one of the rear doors. However, there weren't enough produced and so two of the three trucks only had the decal on the rear. As seen in the photo above. If you look at the truck displayed at the beginning of this chapter you will note that the decal is actually missing from the side of the truck. In the picture above, the truck on the right was the only one that had all of its decals affixed.

The unit also had heavy vests which had patches attached to the front and back of the vest that read 'Housing Police'. Because of the rarity of these particular patches, I have not had the opportunity to examine one up close, but I assume that they conformed roughly to the size of the ESU ones.

Photo courtesy of Dave Kellner.

On April 2, 1995, the NYC Housing Authority Police was consolidated with the New York City Police Department to become the new Housing Bureau and members of the ERU were merged into ESU.

Housing members wore the 5", fully embroidered, regulation Housing Police shoulder patch on the left arm sleeve. The uniform progression was as follows:

- **October 1993** - Light blue uniform shirts with Housing Police patch worn on the left shoulder & Housing ERU patch worn on the right shoulder. Metal breast badges were worn.

- **August 1994** - Dark blue uniform shirts with Housing Police patch worn on the right shoulder & NYPD ESU patch on the left shoulder. NYPD ESU breast patch worn on left pocket. Officer name and housing badge # patch worn on right pocket. NYPD ESU back patch worn on the reverse.

- **April 1995** - Dark blue uniform shirts with NYPD patch worn on the right shoulder & NYPD ESU patch on the left shoulder. NYPD ESU breast patch worn on left pocket. Officer name and NYPD badge # patch worn on right pocket. NYPD ESU back patch worn on the reverse.

NYC TRANSIT POLICE - EMRU

The roots of the NYC Transit Authority Police, Emergency Medical Rescue Unit can be traced back to a Dartmouth University student named Dean Esserman.

In the summer of 1977, while he was in college, Esserman obtained a grant from HELP (the Health Education and Learning Program), which set up an ambulance and emergency unit in the New York City Transit Police Department. Esserman himself would later go on to have an extensive career in law enforcement in New York and Connecticut.

In August of 1977, the original 'arc' patch was authorized for those members of the unit that completed the first  responder course. The 4.25" wide, partially embroidered patch was worn on the right shoulder.

This first patch was a commercially available stock item.

In 1979, Officers Lee Armstrong and Willie Vitola designed a new set of insignia for the unit.

These new patches kept the black and yellow color scheme but incorporated it into a shield shaped design. A large, 3.25", partially embroidered patch size was worn on the right shoulder; while a smaller, 2.25", partially embroidered version was worn on baseball hats.

This style was worn until 1991.

In 1990, William Bratton was selected to become Chief of the Transit Police. In the two years that he was with the agency, he instituted a series of policies designed to improve the department and the morale of its officers.

One of these changes was the redesign of their uniforms, which included the agencies shoulder patch. The roughly 4.5", fully embroidered patch, often referred to as the 'steel dust' patch, was changed from black and yellow to a navy blue and yellow.

As a result of the new uniform changes, the EMRU patches where also modified to reflect this color change as well. While the sizes remained the same, this updated version was fully embroidered. This design remained in use until 1993, when the patch was completely redesigned.

In 1993, a new patch was proposed. The new 3.25", fully embroidered, shield shaped patch featured a train emerging from a tunnel, flanked by the American flag and a medical caduceus.

The decision had been made to remove the word 'medical' from the patch, but when the first version appeared not only had the word 'medical' been removed, but so had the word 'emergency'. The 'Rescue Unit' version was rejected by the unit.

The 2nd issue came out toward the end of 1993. It retained the same size and design elements of the first issue, but this time it featured the title 'Emergency Rescue'. Only a few months after it was adopted, the department would be merged into the NYPD.

When Transit switched to the .9mm it created a rift between them and the NYPD which, under Police Commissioner Raymond Kelly, refused to change from the .38 cal revolvers.

This carried over and caused a rivalry between the NYPD's Firearms Unit, whose unofficial mascot was the Warner Bros. Loony Tunes character, 'Yosemite Sam', and the Transit Firearms unit, which adopted the Warner Brothers 'Tasmanian Devil' character as theirs. This 'feud' then led to a couple of provocative Transit Firearms Unit patches in which they declared themselves as *The Best*.

The use of the Taz chacaretr as the Transit Police unofficial mascot of sorts expanded, and the Emergency Rescue Unit included him into several of their novelty patches as well.

The first ERU appearance of Taz was on a 5", fully embroidered, novelty patch that was produced in early 1993. This featured the character standing on a length of railroad tracks and hoisting a train car above him. He is wearing a Heckler and Koch MP5 submachine gun strapped across his chest and, off to the side, is the familiar Jaws of Life device.

In addition to this design there were two smaller versions produced that were designed to be worn on ball caps. Each features the identical Taz image, but with variations on the lettering. Both versions are partially embroidered, but one is 5" wide while the other is 3" high.

Another patch which, while not an official item, did see limited use on duty jackets, was from a company called Paratech that manufactured lift-bags.

Since one of the primary functions of the Transit EMRU dealt with individuals who had been struck by trains, the EMRU used the Paratech system to jack the trains off the track so that they could extricate the victim.

Eventually, EMRU became so proficient that they reduced the time of lifting a train from a standard of fifteen to twenty minutes down to five or less.

Paratech even used the EMRU training films as part of their sales demos.

On April 2, 1995, the NYC Transit Police was consolidated with the New York City Police Department to become the new Transit Bureau and members of the EMRU were merged into ESU.

UNKNOWN

During my research for this book I encountered several patches that I was unable to explain. I'd reached out to countless members of the units to ask about them, but was never able to get a definitive answer.

I have posted them here because I cannot say, with any measure of certainty, whether they are authentic or fantasy, knowing that there will always be those who seek to benefit from tragedy or the popularity of a particular unit. If anyone could shed some light on them, I would appreciate hearing from you.

The first patch comes from Truck 1. This patch purports to be a memorial insignia done to honor Police Officer Brian McDonnell who was killed during the attack on the World Trade Center on September 11th, 2001.

This 5" design features a Tomcat, leaning on the '1' logo. It is partially embroidered, with a grey twill background.

The second patch is another apparent memorial design to honor the three officers of Truck 2, who were also killed in the attack on September 11th. Their names are listed on the outer border: Sergeant Michael Curtin, Detective Joe Vigiano, and Police Officer John D'Allara.

This 6" design features a slightly altered version of the Truck 2 patch that was done by Detective Vigiano. Rather than using a royal blue which is on the original patch, this design features a brighter, sky blue color. It is also partially embroidered, with a white twill background.

What is interesting about this particular design is that it was apparently copied from a 3-D carved plaque that is on display in Truck 2's quarters.

Artwork courtesy of David Smith, **Phoenix Sign and Design**

After the 9/11 attack, Detective Joe Vigiano's friend, David Smith, who designed the previously discussed patches for Joe, did the plaque for Truck 2 as well as 2 others for the FDNY.

He also produced individual graphics for each of the Truck 2 officers who were killed on 9/11.

Artwork courtesy of David Smith, **Phoenix Sign and Design**

The third patch comes from Truck 4 and has a very interesting story. Back in 2004, Detective Evan Schwerner asked Huntzman Enterprises to come up with a potentially new design for a patch for the unit.

The proposed artwork featured a Tomcat holding a Y-Bar and shotgun. The Tomcat was leaning on the stylized 'NY' logo with a green '4' superimposed over it. While the design was rejected for the patch, it was in fact used as a decal by the unit.

The patch design is almost an identical replica of the proposed design, with only minor changes in the color scheme. None of the current or former members of Truck 4, that I have spoken to, have ever seen the patch.

REPRODUCTIONS

Sadly, I would be remiss if I didn't address this subject, as it was one of the driving forces for writing this book.

Because of the popularity of ESU insignia, it was only a matter of time before reproductions would begin to surface. When you consider that, as of the original writing of this book, many of the truck patches are quickly approaching the thirty year mark. It is not unusual then that the purveyors of fake / reproduction patches would jump on the bandwagon and produce fakes to sell to unsuspecting collectors.

I recall one collector sending me a scan of several older truck patches that he had been assured were real, as they came from an NYPD officer who had purchased them in a police equipment store. It is always hard to find a way to educate people, tactfully, when you have to explain that the majority of their *prized* collections are comprised of reproductions. In fact, up until last year, every truck patch had been reproduced, with the exception of the old Truck 6 'Ram's Head' patch. Sadly, as of this writing, that patch has also fallen victim to the reproducers.

While many of the reproductions originated in the United States, more and more are now coming out of Europe. I know of one police officer in Spain who has spent a large amount of money procuring original patches, only to then take them and have them reproduced. Auction sites provide a safe-haven for these folks to ply their fakes. I have heard several reports of sellers intentionally showing a photo of a legitimate patch on their auction page, but sending the winning bidder a reproduction.

It was my hope that in writing this book I could educate collectors about some of the history and details that could help them navigate the rocky shoals of patch collecting.

I could probably write an entire book just on the reproduction ESU truck patches. I have seen them all, from the *really close* to the just plain *ugly*. At one point I actually toyed with the idea of adding them in, so that collectors could know what to avoid, but decided against it so that I didn't give the reproduction artists an idea of where to 'fix' their mistakes.

The best advice I can give to collectors, who wish to avoid the pitfalls of reproductions, is to make sure that you obtain the items from reputable sources. In the military collecting community there is an old adage that rings true in the law enforcement field as well: *"Buy the item, not the story."*

If someone is offering you an original Staten Island shaped Truck 5 patch, then realize that it is most likely going to be a reproduction. Does that mean you should avoid it altogether? No, because the actual production number was only in the teens, so it might be the only one you will ever get. If they are peddling a story that their *brother's, cousin's, sister's aunt once dated a guy who knew someone in Truck 5* and that's how they got the patch, it might be true, but.....

The one thing we do have going for us, as a collecting community, is that many of the patches done in the 80's and early 90's were manufactured on older machines. They don't have the crisp, commercial look of today's insignia. Fortunately, in an attempt to minimize potential reproductions, a lot of the newer designs coming out have the manufacturer's sticker on the back.

At the end of the day, research and trusted sources are still your best bet to avoid getting burned.

ADDENDUM

"You're never done, and you <u>never</u> stop learning."

The field of collecting and researching ESU insignia is a continually evolving one. Each year new insignia is released, while other, previously unknown ones are discovered. One of the newest areas that I am currently researching is the growing trend of challenge coins and I hope to include a new section devoted to them in a later edition.

In my collection I have several patches, the authenticity of which, I have been unable to verify. I will continue to investigate these and, if I can validate them, I will add them in a later edition.

One of the most frustrating things for me, as a researcher and author, is to have to grudgingly accept the fact that some information will remain elusive, at least for the time being. In reading this book you will have undoubtedly noticed that some patches are clearly attributed, while others are more vague. The reason for this is that, while I may *know* that a particular patch was done by a certain officer, or produced in a certain period of time, I have been hesitant to add this information without corroboration. I think it would be grossly unfair for me to identify someone and then have to do a retraction later. Any new information that is uncovered will be added to future editions.

For those of you who know of patches that should be included, or who have information that would aid to the accuracy of this book, I ask that you to please contact me. I am also interested in any personal photos showing officers wearing insignia and old NYPD, HAPD or TAPD ESU vehicles.

You can find information on how to reach me on my author page at the end of this book.

About the Author

Andrew G. Nelson is a twenty-two year law enforcement veteran and a graduate of the State University of New York. He served twenty years with the New York City Police Department, achieving the rank of sergeant before retiring in 2005.

He is the author of several mystery novels. 'Uncommon Valor: Insignia of the NYPD Emergency Service Unit' is his first non-fiction work.

He and his wife have four children and currently reside with their Irish Wolfhound in central Illinois.

For more information please visit:

http://andrewgnelson.blogspot.com/

Like us on Facebook:

https://www.facebook.com/pages/Andrew-Nelson/168310343376572